What people are saying about …

AHA

"Kyle knows where we live and where we could live with God's help. He is committed to helping us move in the right direction. If you need a helping hand in your journey, he'll point you to the right Person."

Max Lucado, pastor of Oak Hills
Church and author of *Grace*

"Kyle will challenge you to grow from a fair-weather fan to a full-time follower of Christ."

Craig Groeschel, senior pastor of
LifeChurch.tv and author of *Fight*

"Kyle will challenge even the most obedient Christians to relook at their relationship with Christ."

Mike Huckabee, former governor of
Arkansas and bestselling author

"Like his preaching, Kyle's writings will bring you face-to-face with areas you need to change and the One who has the power to change you."

Dave Stone, senior pastor of Southeast Christian Church
and author of *Raising Your Kids to Love the Lord*

"Fresh, insightful, practical—Kyle's writing and teaching are helping countless people. I'm thrilled with how God is using him to challenge and encourage both Christians and those who are checking out the faith. Count me among his many fans!"

Lee Strobel, bestselling author and professor at Houston Baptist University

"*AHA* outlines biblical transformation and how it works in a simple yet profound way. Do you want to change, improve, or grow? You must get this book!"

Mark Batterson, lead pastor of National Community Church and *New York Times* bestselling author of *All In*

"Kyle cuts through all the nonsense and takes us straight to what is most important spiritually."

Jud Wilhite, senior pastor of Central Christian Church and author of *The God of Yes*

"If you're minimizing just how bad things have gotten in your life or are simply ready to change for good, then *AHA* awaits. This book is a gut punch to passivity. A bombshell to procrastination. Don't hold back now. Embrace the startling realization in these pages, talk straight with your soul, and take immediate action. Your gracious, loving Father stands ready for you."

Caleb Breakey, author of *Called to Stay* and *Dating Like Airplanes*

"Kyle is a great communicator, always driving home his messages in powerful, compelling, and practical ways."

David Novak, CEO of YUM! Brands (Taco Bell, Pizza Hut, KFC) and author of *Taking People with You*

AHA

AWAKENING.HONESTY.ACTION

STUDENT EDITION

THE GOD MOMENT THAT
CHANGES EVERYTHING

kyle idleman

David C Cook®

transforming lives together

AHA: STUDENT EDITION
Published by David C Cook
4050 Lee Vance View
Colorado Springs, CO 80918 U.S.A.

David C Cook Distribution Canada
55 Woodslee Avenue, Paris, Ontario, Canada N3L 3E5

David C Cook U.K., Kingsway Communications
Eastbourne, East Sussex BN23 6NT, England

The graphic circle C logo is a registered trademark of David C Cook.

The website addresses recommended throughout this book are offered as a
resource to you. These websites are not intended in any way to be or imply an
endorsement on the part of David C Cook, nor do we vouch for their content.

LCCN 2014901070
ISBN 978-0-7814-1144-8
eISBN 978-0-7814-1165-3

© 2014 Kyle Idleman
Published in association with the literary agency of The
Gates Group, www.the-gates-group.com.

The Team: Alex Field, Amy Konyndyk, Nick Lee, Tonya Osterhouse, Karen Athen
Cover Design: Amy Konyndyk
Cover Photo: Matt Garmany and Jennifer Wollen

Printed in the United States of America
First Edition 2014

1 2 3 4 5 6 7 8 9 10

013114

CONTENTS

Chapter 1

THE DISTANT COUNTRY

Artificial grass.

Sugar-free candy.

Powdered milk.

There are some words that just shouldn't go together. They even have a weird name. Think back to that English class. Remember? They're called oxymorons.

Want some more? *Bittersweet, jumbo shrimp, silent alarm, invisible ink.* How about *Twitter conversation*? Sometimes oxymorons may be less obvious, like *plastic glasses, Microsoft Works,* or *cheerleading scholarship*.[1] But one oxymoron that's often used and easily missed is *self-help*.

Quick tip: don't ask where the self-help section is when you're at the bookstore. You're better off finding it yourself. I once made the mistake of inquiring. The store clerk, who had looked dazed and bored out of his mind a second earlier, suddenly perked up.

---

1. Sorry, cheerleaders. Couldn't resist.

He looked me over for a few seconds, trying—I think—to tell exactly what parts of my self needed help. I didn't appreciate the scrutiny. Finally he pointed me toward a section in the back. I say "section," but really it was like an entire region. A fourth of the store was dedicated to all manner of self-help guides. It was a little overwhelming.

So I perused the aisles, suddenly feeling as though there was a lot wrong with me. There were books like *How to Make People Like You in 90 Seconds or Less*, *How to Get a Girlfriend*, and *How to Get Your Boyfriend Back*. The books contained all sorts of plans and covered topics from clean teeth and fresh breath to making small talk and dating more than one guy or girl at once. Then there were titles like *Becoming a Better You*; *You Are Why You Eat*; *Act Like a Lady, Think Like a Man*; and *How to Get What You Want*. I quickly fled the self-help section with new doubts about my mental and physical health nipping at my heels.[2]

No matter the subject—did I mention it seemed like there was a whole warehouse full?—all of these books promised a new and improved version of my life in a few easy steps. It's hard not to be cynical, because logically speaking, if one of the books worked, the rest of them wouldn't be necessary. But the truth is, self-help books that promise guaranteed, can't-fail, new-and-improved changes are everywhere.

An article in *New York* magazine reported that the self-help movement has mushroomed into an "$11 billion industry

---

2. Okay, I confess. I bought *3 Jedi Mind Tricks for Street Fighters*. You got a problem with that? (Mind Trick number 1: Be an Aggressor.)

dedicated to telling us how to improve our lives."[3] The article observed that there are at least forty-five thousand self-help books in print.

But most of us would have to admit that our self still needs help. Check out the options on your e-reader. You'll find lists of selections on the following topics: Diet and exercise; improving your relationships; getting control of your finances or getting rich; stress management; and overcoming addictions. And that's just a few. Look a little closer, and you'll see that no matter the topic, all of these books have similar taglines and formulas. It's like all the authors were at the same Mad Libs party.

> *Follow our* [NUMBER 1–8] *easy steps, and we guarantee you will* [INSERT FINANCIAL GAIN, WEIGHT LOSS GOAL, OR RELATIONAL STATUS] *in only a matter of* [NUMBER 1–5] [INSERT A MEASUREMENT OF TIME].

And because we're all too aware that our self needs help, we jump on this misery merry-go-round and buy book after book, hoping for better results. We know something is wrong. We even know what we want to change. Our diagnosis is spot-on, but no medication seems to do the trick.

So if you picked up this book because you are trying to help yourself make some significant changes, I want to tell you up front

---

3. Kathryn Schulz, "The Self in Self-Help," *New York*, January 6, 2013, nymag.com /health/self-help/2013/schulz-self-searching/.

that this isn't the book for you. If self could help, then we would all
have been fixed a long time ago.

Let me be clear: AHA is not a self-help process. This is the
antithesis of a self-help book. What Bizarro is to Superman,[4] this
book is to the self-help genre. This journey begins by rejecting self's
offer to help.

AHA: Spiritual Transformation

The word *aha* is actually in the dictionary. This is roughly defined as
"when something is suddenly seen, found, or understood." We'll talk
about it as AHA: "a sudden spiritual understanding, recognition, or
resolution that brings about lasting transformation." Instead of self-
help, we are asking for God's help. AHA is a spiritual experience that
brings about supernatural change.

In some ways AHA can't be explained—it must be experienced.
That's why it's best understood through stories. AHA is that moment
in someone's life where there is a beautiful collision. At just the right
time, there is a "God moment" when life collides with God's Word
and the power of the Holy Spirit.

Everything changes during that collision. Watching that
change is one of my favorite parts of being a pastor. I love witness-
ing AHA. I see it most weekends at the church where I serve. I

---

4. If this reference doesn't make sense to you, try one of the following: what PC
   is to Mac, what the Joker is to Batman, what Sonic is to the Raw Food Diet,
   what Peeta is to Gale, what Sauron is to Frodo, what shirts are to Matthew
   McConaughey.

listen to people tell about the spiritual awakening they have experienced. They were lost, but now they are found. They were blind, but now they can see.

One girl told about trying to cope with life through impulsive eating. There was nothing a day could throw at her that she couldn't eat away. A stressful week of classes would lead to a weekend of third and fourth helpings. Facing anxiety from an upcoming project, she would bring home two or three desserts and eat them all at once. Sure, she tried every diet and exercise fad, but she reached 325 pounds. Her weight gain felt unstoppable, and she sank into a deep depression, which only worsened her eating habits. Finally after months and months of cycling through depression and binging, she realized something: food was never going to fill the emptiness in her heart. She had been trying to satisfy her soul by feeding her stomach.

When she came to church, she heard me talk about John 6, the place in the Bible where Jesus described Himself as the "Bread of Life." In that moment, this girl realized she had been turning to food for what, ultimately, only Jesus could do for her. That was four years and 170 pounds ago. But the outward change was just a by-product of the inner transformation she experienced. She started to look to Jesus to fill the emptiness of her heart.

AHA.

Another girl realized only Jesus could take away the pain that had driven her to cutting.

AHA.

A guy found that only Jesus could free him from the pornography habit he'd become slave to.

AHA.

Three Essential Ingredients

So what is AHA?

My wife has this cookbook at home, a gift from our wedding. It's called *The Three Ingredient Cookbook*. She would want me to tell you that she doesn't really use it. She typically uses more than three ingredients when she cooks. The truth is I'm the one who uses *The Three Ingredient Cookbook*. On the rare occasions I'm allowed in the kitchen, this cookbook is my go-to cooking companion, because honestly, three ingredients is about all I can handle. One of the things I've learned the hard way is that when you use *The Three Ingredient Cookbook*, all three ingredients are necessary. This is the downside to *The Three Ingredient Cookbook*. You can't cheat. If you only use two ingredients, the dish doesn't turn out very well.

The same is true for AHA. I have listened to the AHA experiences of hundreds—if not thousands—of people over the years. I have studied the transformation experiences of people in the Bible. And I have found that there is amazing consistency—AHA always has three ingredients. If any one of these ingredients is missing, it short-circuits the transformation process.

Here are the three ingredients:

1. A Sudden Awakening
2. Brutal Honesty
3. Immediate Action

Those three elements are always necessary for AHA to take place. If there is an awakening and honesty but no action, then AHA doesn't happen. If there is awakening and action but no honesty, AHA won't last. But when God's Word and the Holy Spirit bring these three things together in your life, you will experience AHA.

The AHA Parable

The three ingredients of AHA really stand out in Jesus's most famous parable: the parable of the prodigal son. Ask friends who have never even opened a Bible, and they probably know this story. You—and they—can find it in Luke 15. Let's travel with the Prodigal Son on his journey. We'll see the three elements of AHA in his life, and we can pray for them in our own.

In the story, a father had two sons. The youngest son came to his father and insisted on getting his share of the inheritance—immediately. He was ready to leave home and head out on his own.

Jesus said the son ended up in "a distant country" (Luke 15:13). Remember, Jesus was telling this parable to Jewish leaders. When he used the phrase *distant country*, they knew exactly what he meant. Back then, any distant land would be considered Gentile land, which was a big deal. It clearly meant the son wasn't just walking away from his father; he was walking away from his faith.

Bound for the Distant Country

Every AHA story includes the Distant Country—areas of our lives where we leave God out. We post No Trespassing signs around the perimeter and make it clear that God is not welcome.

Like the Prodigal Son, we leave the Father's house and head out on our own.

It may help to pause and think about your life. What are the areas of your life—or maybe it's your whole life—that could be described as the Distant Country? Take a minute and replace this general description—Distant Country—with the name of your own specific location. You can even write it here:

There are a lot of reasons why we leave the Father and head for the Distant Country.

The Prodigal Son was consumed with *now* and wasn't too concerned with *later*. He wanted his money immediately even though he would have gotten more if he waited. The cravings for immediate pleasure squandered what would have been a life-changing investment. But the son had more greed than patience, and he took what he shouldn't have even been asking for and headed off. When he arrived in the distant country, he wasted his money on "wild living." He didn't care about saving anything for later. He was only into getting as much pleasure as he could at the moment.

It reminds me of the 2013 Super Bowl—or the Super Bowl commercials anyway. Those are the best part, right? Pepsi's advertising campaign in 2013 was hard to miss. After all, they ran multiple thirty-second spots and sponsored the halftime show. Their slogan was simple: Live for Now.

Pepsi spent millions of dollars communicating that message. I think they could have saved themselves a lot of money; that message is unnecessary. "Live for Now" is what most of us do best. It's our default approach to life. The word that best captures Pepsi's motto is *hedonism*. Not quite as catchy as "Live for Now," but that's essentially hedonism's definition. It's the heart of wild living. Hedonists don't worry about what happens later or what consequences they may face down the road.

This was the Prodigal Son's approach to life: live for now *now* and worry about later *later*. Whatever might happen later didn't seem nearly as important as what he might experience right now.

The Distant Country is the land where you live for now, and later find your self is in desperate need of help. If you think about the different areas of your self that need some help, there's a good chance that choosing to "Live for Now" is what got your self in trouble in the first place.

When you travel to the Distant Country, you are not just *going*—you are also *leaving*. The Prodigal Son went for wild living, but he also left his father. What drives many travelers to the Distant Country is that, for one reason or another, they are running away from God. Everyone who runs from God has his or her own reason, but there are a few common reasons prodigals pack their bags and turn their backs away from the Father's house.

The Unreasonable Father

The son in Luke 15 seemed to think that living in his father's house has caused him to miss out. Similarly, many travelers to the Distant Country also see God as an unreasonable Father. In this light, we see God as a Father who has a long list of rules that seem designed to take all the fun out of life. These travelers might describe God as "The Great Cosmic Killjoy" who's out to ruin any fun.

That's probably how Justin would have described God. Justin grew up in a Christian home and attended a Christian school. His parents forced him to keep his hair short and his curfew early. Justin was convinced that his sheltered life had caused him to miss out. One year, Justin was home watching *MTV Spring Break* thinking about all the fun he should be having. So as soon as he graduated from high school, he packed his bags and headed for the Distant Country. What else would you expect from a son who spent years in the Father's house daydreaming about all the fun he was missing out on?

The Unpleasable Father

Others head for the Distant Country because they see God as an unpleasable Father. The rationale goes something like this: because God's standards are so high, nothing I do will ever be good enough for Him. Maybe these people grew up in a church that influenced this belief—whenever they heard about God, He always seemed frustrated with them. Maybe everything they heard about God made them believe that He would only shake His head in disappointment whenever He looked at them.

Or maybe they grew up feeling like their best was never good enough. If they brought home a B on their report card, it should have been an A. If they scored fifteen points during the basketball game, they should've had twenty.

If you think of God as an unpleasable Father, at some point you'll quit trying. What's the point of making the effort if nothing you do is good enough?

The Unmerciful Father

Some leave the Father and head for the Distant Country because they see God as an unmerciful Father. They see God as an angry Father who is borderline abusive and who seems to find pleasure in distributing punishment. He's always watching and waiting for them to slip up. And when He catches them, it doesn't matter how sorry they are—there will be hell to pay ... literally.

If you've been taught to be afraid of God, you'll naturally respond by running away from Him.

A few years ago I came home from work to find that my wife and kids had agreed to dog-sit for some friends. The dog's name was Pork Chop, and everyone was excited about our new house-guest. But when I walked into the room, Pork Chop was not glad to see me. He responded to my presence by peeing on the floor and running into the next room. I tried not to take it personally, but later that same evening, when I walked into the room where Pork Chop was, he responded the same way. He peed, ran away, and hid.

We later found out that Pork Chop had been rescued from an abusive situation and had learned to be afraid of men. He had no reason to fear me. I had taken him into my home and provided him with shelter and food. But because Pork Chop had learned to be afraid of men, he always ran away. I could never get close to him.

That's how some people relate to God.[5] They run away to the Distant Country and never give Him a chance, because they've been conditioned to be afraid of Him.

The Uncaring Father

I wish it weren't so common, but I've talked to many travelers who are in the Distant Country because they see God as an uncaring Father. *God wasn't there for me when I needed Him the most,* they think. So they head to the Distant Country and don't look back. From then on, they view God as an impersonal force that doesn't know or care about what's happening in their lives. So their relationship with God can be summed up like this: if He doesn't care about me, then I don't care about Him.

Family therapist John Trent shared a letter given to him by a third-grade teacher. The letter was part of a school assignment. The students had been told to write a letter to their fathers. Here's what one student wrote:

Dear Daddy, I love you so much. When are you going to come see me again? I miss you very much. I love when you take me to the pool. When am I going to spend the night at your house? Have you ever seen my house before? I want to see what your house looks like. When am I going to get to see you again? I love you, Daddy.

---

5. Minus the peeing.

What's going to happen to that third grader's heart as she gets older? She will become more disillusioned and disappointed. Eventually she'll walk away bitter and wounded.

The Loving Father

What we discover in Jesus's parable is that God is a loving, merciful, gracious, and caring Father. When we end up in the Distant Country, it's inevitable that we will find ourselves in a place where self is in desperate need of help. And where we turn for that help can make all the difference.

You heard the beginning of Justin's story—the kid who was watching MTV and itching to have some fun. He headed to the Distant Country and dove in to wild living completely: sex, booze, parties, all-nighters. And Justin was the wildest when it came to drugs. You name it; Justin tried it. Didn't matter how extreme or how dangerous, Justin was always ready to get high.

But after a while, the drugs that were fun became an addiction, and addiction brought Justin to his knees. His life was in shambles, and Justin knew he needed something. He made some noble self-help attempts, but each tearful resolution always ended in relapse. He tried to get professional help. Rehab treatments failed, addiction cleanses didn't stick, and working a program never worked. Justin started to feel like he had nowhere to turn. A horrifying notion awoke inside of him: *Maybe I'm broken for good.*

Justin recently came to speak with me after one of our weekend church services. "I'm high on heroine right now," were the first words out of his mouth. Looking into his sunken face and bloodshot eyes, I believed him. He began to weep as he told me his story. It seems that his reckless choices had left a trail of emotional wreckage that had wounded his relationships with friends, family, and, ultimately, God.

But Justin was realizing that God wasn't a Father who wanted to ruin life's fun. He was a Father who loved him and would forgive him no matter what. Justin felt he needed to get help *that instant*, because he couldn't trust himself to wait the twenty-four hours till Monday morning. He looked at me, shaken with his own reality and desperate for help. I embraced him, and all I could say was, "You've come to the right place."

The AHA journey doesn't begin with a determined commitment to self-help—it starts with a humble request for God's help. Justin learned a simple truth that changed everything: when there's nowhere else to turn, all you have to do is turn around and head back to the Father. Justin summed it up by saying, "I'm tired of running from God."

AHA.

PART 1
SUDDEN AWAKENING

When he came to his senses ...

Chapter 2

COMING TO YOUR SENSES

What's your morning alarm? I use my phone,[1] and not long ago, one of my daughters changed my alarm tone to one that features her favorite animal. It's labeled "Horses Neighing." It should be called "Death by Stampede." At 5:30 in the morning, my alarm went off, and I shot straight up in bed, wide-awake and sure I was about to be trampled by wild mustangs.

While I was changing it back to my standard alarm, I noticed the wide array of options. If you use an iPhone, go ahead and pull it out.[2] "Doorbell" is just confusing. *What? Is someone here to see me?* And "Harp" practically sings, "Go back to sleep. It's the right thing

---

1. Some of you think that's a little risky, but that's because you're Android users. If you had an iPhone, you wouldn't worry about it. Just sayin'.

2. I'm sure you Android users have options, too, so go ahead and check those out.

to do. Your teacher will understand." That's exactly what I would do if "Harp" were my alarm tone.

"Old Car Horn" is the most effective alarm for me. If you don't have an iPhone, think of a security alarm that you can hear on the other side of the neighborhood—and that you're sleeping inside the security alarm's speaker. It's highly effective. And if the alarm doesn't get me out of bed immediately, its unique backup system kicks into gear—literally. My wife's foot slams into the small of my back, pushing me out of bed to shut the alarm off.

But here's what I've discovered: the more you don't want to hear it, the more effective the alarm is.

Until your desire to silence the alarm outweighs your desire to keep sleeping, you're not going to wake up.

Waking Up

A sudden awakening takes place when God finally gets our attention. The alarm sounds, and this time we hear it. The alarm causes us to sit up and get out of bed. We are suddenly very aware of our present circumstances and the reality that something must change. Even though we've traveled far from the Father and are living in the Distant Country, we are awake to reality like never before. This is the first ingredient of AHA: a sudden awakening. In Jesus's story, the Prodigal Son experienced a sudden awakening "when he came to his senses" (Luke 15:17).

Like being awoken from a deep sleep when the fire alarm goes off, the Prodigal Son was jolted awake. He sat straight up and suddenly realized what his life had become. He wondered how things turned out this way. He had never imagined it would come to this when he left his father's house. It was never part of the plan. But life got his attention in a harsh way, and he knew things had to change. One moment he was sleeping; the next he was awake. AHA.

Have you had a moment like this:

She read the text again: "Pick u up at the corner. No one's home." She knew what he meant. Her phone buzzed again, and she jumped. The message was from another friend: "Haven't seen u in a while. U doin ok?"

The alarm sounded.

Or a moment like one of these:

He ran out the back door when the cops busted the party, but this time, they were there, too.

She was a junior in high school. With trembling hands she held a pregnancy test, waiting for the result.

He logged off the website, deleted his history, and turned off the computer just as his mom called his name.

Her mom pulled up her sleeves and asked about the angry red cuts.

Sooner or later in the Distant Country, the alarm goes off.

Heavy Sleeper

The Prodigal Son in Jesus's story didn't hear the alarm until he made it all the way to the pigpen. He didn't hear it when he asked his father for his inheritance. He didn't hear it when his wallet was lighter after only a few raging weekends in the distant country. He didn't hear it when a famine swept through the land. He didn't even hear it when he found himself applying for a job as a pig-sitter. It's hard not to read this story and ask, "How did he not hear it? How could he sleep through that?"

We often miss the alarms sounding in our lives, because we're not sensitive to them. "Harp" won't do the job. It's going to take "Death by Stampede" to wake us up. So instead of responding to the alarm early on, we hit snooze—and we keep hitting snooze until the alarm grows so loud and unpleasant that it can't be ignored. Then we wake up, rub our eyes, and notice that pigs surround us. And we wonder, *How did it come to this?*

Are some alarms sounding in your life right now?

God often sounds the alarm early on to wake us up before things have fallen apart. Sometimes people think they have to hit rock bottom before they come to their senses. But what if God is trying to wake you up right now to save you from heartbreak in the Distant Country later?

God is a loving Father. The moment a parent senses a child might be in danger, he or she warns the child of what's coming. I do it with my kids. Your parents probably still do it with you.[3]

A few years ago my family was visiting my parents for the holidays. They live on a quiet cul-de-sac, and cars rarely drive by. So my then-four-year-old son, Kael, was riding a Big Wheel down the driveway. I stepped outside and saw a car coming down the street pretty fast. Kael didn't see the car coming; he needed to be warned. I didn't think, *I've got a good thirty seconds before that car makes contact with*

---

3. You might wish they'd quit it. But try to cut them some slack. It's like a protection gene kicks in when your child is born.

my son—that's enough time to check my texts before I say something. I didn't smile and say, "Hey, buddy, there's a Ford SUV coming right for you. You might want to think about slowing down." No, I yelled, "Kael, stop right now!" As soon as I perceived the danger, I warned him. That's what a loving father does.

Here are some of the ways God sounds the alarm:

God's Word at Just the Right Time

God sounded the first individual, timely alarm in Genesis, the first book of the Bible. Adam and Eve had two sons at the time: Cain and Abel. Abel was a shepherd. Cain was a farmer. And they both brought offerings to God. The Bible says, "The LORD looked with favor on Abel and his offering, but on Cain and his offering he did not look with favor. So Cain was very angry, and his face was downcast" (Gen. 4:4–5).

So what was the deal?

Abel obeyed God's command and brought the best he had. But Cain gave God leftovers. He collected whatever crops had been left on the ground and gave that to God as his offering.

God accepted Abel's offering and blessed him. But He didn't want Cain's scraps. Cain got jealous and angry; the world's first son was on the prodigal path to the Distant Country. But God saw what was happening and sounded the alarm. He said to Cain, "Why are you angry? Why is your face downcast? If you do what is right, will you not be accepted?" (Gen. 4:6–7).

God, as a Father, said, "Listen—it's not too late. I know you're feeling discouraged. I know my response wasn't what you wanted. I know things haven't really turned out the way you had hoped, but *it's not too late*. You still have an opportunity to do the right thing. If you'll do the right thing, even though you don't feel like it, everything will be okay."

Then God gave a second alarm. He said, "But if you do not do what is right, sin is crouching at your door; it desires to have you, but you must rule over it" (Gen. 4:7).

Here's the phrase I want to highlight: *sin is crouching at your door*. God painted a word picture of Cain getting ready to open a door. If he opened it, he would be making a decision that would destroy his family and devastate his life. God the Father saw the first son going toward the door, and He put a heavy hand on the door. He held it shut for a minute and said, "Now wait a minute, Cain. Push Pause. You need to take a deep breath and recognize something. What is right behind this door, what you're about to come face-to-face with, has the power to destroy. It's hunting you down. Cain, be really careful about what you do next."

The alarm was sounding, but God stepped back and let Cain choose for himself. Just like the Prodigal Son's father, God wasn't going to force His child to make the right decision. Every parent knows that kids eventually have to decide for themselves.

Cain ignored the alarm and opened the door. He invited his brother out into a field and killed him.

God had warned Cain early on, but Cain sleepwalked through the alarm. He did what he wanted to do. And everything came crashing down around Cain.

In hindsight, most of us can identify moments like that in our lives—moments when God sounded the alarm but we rolled over and went back to sleep. As I have listened to people's AHA stories over the years, I often ask, "Looking back on it, can you see some ways that God was trying to get your attention but you just didn't realize it?"

I am completely convinced that part of the supernatural power of God's words in the Bible is that they often intersect with our lives when we are most desperate for the truth. Like a GPS that gives us a heads-up when our exit is quickly approaching, God uses the Bible to speak into our lives right when we need it the most.

The Words of Someone in Your Life

The words of someone close to us can be an effective alarm. The Prodigal Son needed a friend like this, but that kind of friend is hard to find in the Distant Country. The Bible's book of wisdom, Proverbs, says, "Wounds from a friend can be trusted" (Prov. 27:6). Sometimes a familiar voice speaking truth into our lives is exactly what we need—especially in emergency situations. We may not always want to hear it, but the words need to be said. And be listened to.

Do you have a friend, family member, or youth leader who asks about the guys or girls you date? Does someone keep tabs on your Internet activity?

Are you willing to be honest with this person? Do you listen when they sound an alarm?

I learned early on that some people sitting in church won't hear what I have to say about spiritual firestorms headed their way. If you're one of those people and won't listen to a preacher, then I pray you will listen to a close friend, family member, teacher, or small-group leader who will warn you about potential dangers in your life.

Not long ago I needed someone like this in my life. I came to work wearing an outfit I had convinced myself would still pass for cool: a red polo shirt, pleated khaki pants, and white Nikes. As soon as I walked into the office, one of my friends took a quick glance at me and said, "Hey, Zack Morris, how do you like working at Target?" Now whenever my fashion choices revert back to the early '90s, he just calls me Zack.[4] We all need a friend like that from time to time.

A Taste of Future Consequences

Sometimes God will let us get a sampling of the consequences that will come if we continue down the path we're on. It might hurt a little, but not nearly as bad as it could. Think of it as a fender bender in a parking lot. It'll leave a mark, but not as much as a fiery five-car pileup on the interstate would. In a way, this kind of alarm is like a real-life movie trailer that gives you highlights—or lowlights in this case—of what's coming.

The danger is thinking that we just got lucky. *Phew, dodged that one,* we think, and dismiss it as an inconvenient coincidence. If our sampled consequence isn't big enough or painful enough to get our

---

4. Okay, you millennials, here's a quick lesson in Gen-X TV. You've probably seen cable reruns of *Saved by the Bell.* You can actually evaluate bad fashion by using the entire cast of that early '90s classic. If someone is wearing stonewashed pleated jeans, you can call them A. C. Slater. If their pants are too high and their shirts are too loud, you can call them Screech Powers. If their bangs are too big and standing straight up, use Kelly Kapowski as their nickname. If they are twenty years old and dress like they're fifty, you can call them Lisa Turtle, and if they annoy you no matter what they're wearing, you can call them Jessie Spano.

full attention, we often miss it. But as you look back on your life, I bet you can point out times when God was trying to get your attention. There was probably at least one small-scale issue that foreshadowed a future disaster, and you didn't take heed.

Have you ever seen the A&E reality series *Beyond Scared Straight*? The idea came from a documentary that was filmed in the late 1970s. The concept is to take teenage juvenile offenders—sixteen-year-old car thieves, high-school vandals, repeat-offender shoplifters, drug dealers, etc.—and put them in prison for a day. The idea sounded a little cruel to me at first, but then I watched the teens being interviewed *before* they went into the prison. Many were obnoxiously arrogant. They grinned and bragged about how easy their day would be. In interviews, police officers told producers how these kids thought prison actually sounded nice, like they could eat, sleep, and hang out all day for free.

The teens quickly discovered a different reality. They put on orange jumpsuits and walked past the iron bars and worked prison jobs, like dishwashing and scrubbing toilets, and they interacted with some truly terrifying convicts. The cameras zoomed in on the teens' faces, and I could see them starting to come to their senses. The alarm was sounding, and most of them were starting to hear it.

The show has received some criticism, but I think we can all agree that one hard day in prison now is better than years behind bars later. It turns out that most of the kids on the show *do* seem to be scared into changing their ways. Less than 10 percent of the cast from the original documentary ended up in prison again. But there are those who ended up in orange jumpsuits as convicted felons doing hard time. And there are those on the current show who remain defiant and hardened and who are certainly headed for a future behind bars. How can they not hear such a loud, clanging wake-up call?

How can we not?

The Bible tells the story of a famous repeat offender in the Old Testament book of Exodus: the pharaoh of Egypt. Moses told Pharaoh, "This is what the LORD says: 'Let my people go'" (Exod. 8:1). Pharaoh had a chance to say yes to God—instead he hardened his heart and said no. So God turned the land's water to blood, and Moses returned with the same message: "Okay, Pharaoh. Now as God has already said, 'Let my people go.'" You'd think Pharaoh would have gotten a good enough taste of the consequences of refusing God's request, but he was one hard-hearted ruler. "No way," he replied again.

This pattern went on for nine more awful, miserable, suffering-inducing plagues. But instead of granting Israel's freedom, Pharaoh shrank his heart to be smaller than the Grinch's even though it cost him and his people more and more pain.

Pharaoh's story shows us one of the most dangerous side effects of hitting the snooze on the alarm: the more you do it, the louder and more uncomfortable the alarm becomes. How severe do consequences have to get before you finally wake up?

The Example of Others Before Us

If you can learn from others' mistakes, you can save yourself a lot of potential pain. The Bible includes many stories of people who got it wrong and suffered the consequences. Cain was one of them. He lived near the beginning of recorded history, but his name shows up several times in the New Testament. In other words, the early church used Cain as an alarm to wake up and see what not to do. John wrote, "Do not be like Cain, who belonged to the evil one and murdered his brother" (1 John 3:12). He didn't tiptoe around the facts.

The Bible is always surprisingly candid about people who ended up in the Distant Country. Their loss can be our gain. We can hear Cain's alarm and change the path we are on. And when we witness what others experience away from the Father's house—in the past or the present—it's an alarm inviting us to come to our senses before we go any further.

Seeing Your Future

Years ago I took my family on a mission trip to the Dominican Republic. One of the challenges my wife and I faced was keeping our daughter away from the wild dogs that roamed the streets. What squirrels are to America, dogs are to the Dominican Republic. My daughter, who was in second grade at the time, is the ultimate animal lover, and she could not keep her hands off them. We'd walk through a market, and I'd turn around to see her petting a mangy, wild mutt. I often had to scoop her up in my arms before she could stick out her cheek for disease-filled doggy kisses.

We tried to be strict to help our daughter understand how serious this was. We punished her. But my little girl couldn't help herself. She was especially drawn to the sickly looking dogs that had open wounds and flea-ridden scabs. One night she said, "Dad, after we help all the people, can we help the dogs? I want to buy some bandages so we can fix them up." The dogs were breaking her heart, but there was a serious danger to them that she was failing to recognize.

I knew I had to do something to get her attention. She wasn't listening to my warnings, and she was more concerned about the wounded dogs than about what might happen to her. So I went online and found videos of kids who were in the hospital because they'd been bitten by rabid dogs. The images were graphic and sobering. I brought my daughter over to the laptop and showed her the clips.[5]

"Look. I've talked to you about this. I've warned you about these dogs," I told her. "You've been getting in trouble for it, but you're still not staying away from them. You need to see what happened to other kids who did what you're doing."

As she watched the video, I could see it in her eyes. The alarm was finally waking her up. There's something about seeing someone else experience consequences for the same kind of decisions we're making that usually causes us to come to our senses.

If you are on the path to the Distant Country, step back and ask yourself, "Where is this leading? What's happened to others who have gone this way?" How has it worked out for the classmate who tried to cheat on an exam? How has it worked out for the friend who thought smoking a little weed was no big deal? How has it worked out for the sorority sister who said she had her drinking under control? How has it worked out for the girl who thought he'd never show that picture to anyone else? How has it worked out for that celebrity who thought he could fool around without his wife finding out?

---

5. As you get older, you'll realize that this was a questionable parenting tactic. But it worked!

Their consequences serve as a warning to you: if you keep going down this path, you could end up in the same place.

Prayer for the Sleeping to Awake

One of my favorite stories in the Bible is about a prophet named Elisha. You can read it in 2 Kings, but here's the summary: The king of Aram, an enemy of Israel, sent a great army to surround one of Israel's cities and destroy God's prophet Elisha. When they attacked, Elisha and his servant were surrounded. The servant was terrified—go figure. "Master! What are we going to do?" he cried—my guess is with a sense of panic. Elisha's answer was awesome. "Don't be afraid," the prophet answered. "Those who are with us are more than those who are with them" (2 Kings 6:16). Elisha's servant knew he himself was delirious with fear, but he must have thought his master had totally lost all sense of reality. He looked around—and there was no one else with them. They were alone. It was two against an army. But then Elisha prayed a simple prayer for his servant: "Open his eyes, LORD, so that he may see."

What happened next is amazing. "The LORD opened the servant's eyes, and he looked and saw the hills full of horses and chariots of fire all around Elisha" (2 Kings 6:17). The servant's eyes were opened and AHA! He suddenly realized heavenly forces were protecting them. There was nothing to fear.

Elisha's prayer for his servant is my prayer for you today.

God, open her eyes and let her see that even though he walked out on her, you will never leave her. She is not alone.

God, open his eyes so he can see parents who are hurting, too, but who love him beneath their own brokenness.

God, open his eyes and let him see that living to impress others and glorify himself is leading to emptiness.

God, open her eyes and let her see that the right labels and the right styles have become more important than the beauty You have created and want to fulfill inside her.

God, open his eyes and let him see the single mom who lives next door with a young son who doesn't know how to throw a football.

God, open our eyes and let us see the hungry and the hurting who live just a few miles down the road.

God, open our eyes and let us see that what we watch and call *entertainment* is what You died on the cross for.

God, open our eyes and let us see the pride that has blinded us … the sin that has hardened us … and the lies that have deceived us.

Lord, we pray for AHA. Awaken us.

Chapter 3

A DESPERATE MOMENT

What comes to mind when you hear the phrase *rude awakening*? Maybe you've been jolted out of sleep by your phone ringing in the middle of the night only to find out it was a wrong number. Or maybe you've woken with your dog's slobbery tongue panting millimeters from your face. Or maybe you, like me, have wasted some good time on YouTube. That's where rude awakenings go to a whole new level.

Here are some of my favorite rude awakenings:

Shaving cream and a feather
Hot sauce on the lips
Blanket exchanged for a roll of Bubble Wrap
Air horn and Silly String
Saran wrapped to the bed

Hot wax and a shirtless, hairy man sleeping on his stomach[1]

Whether you love pranking your friends and annoying siblings with rude awakenings or hate rude awakenings because you're always the one getting rudely awoken, you've got to agree: they are effective. One second the person was sound asleep. The next, they're wide-awake.

But what do they have to do with AHA?

We saw the Prodigal Son head off to a distant country. He lived wildly away from his father. I'm sure initially he was having a good time.

But eventually life lived apart from his father fell apart. It got hard. One minute, life was a nonstop party. The next, the Prodigal Son was just trying to stay alive. He ran out of money, and then there was a famine in the land. He got so desperate that the scraps and slop the pigs were eating made his mouth water. Only at that moment did he come to his senses.

Life's challenges and problems have a way of getting our attention. Sometimes the only thing that will wake us up is a rude awakening.

I Stopped Running from God When ...

I asked my Facebook friends to finish this sentence for me: *I stopped running from God when* ... Here are some of the responses I got:

---

1. Fine, go ahead and watch a few. But when you find yourself watching "The Evolution of Dance" for the thirty-seventh time, let that be a reminder that you were reading this book.

I stopped running from God when …

… it became clear that I had made a mess of things.

… I hit rock bottom.

… I heard myself say, "I'm an alcoholic."

… people found out about my secret.

… the pregnancy test came back positive.

… the path I was on came to a dead end.

… I woke up in a hospital after an overdose.

… I was in the back of a police car.

… I got fired.

… the affair was discovered.

… I realized I had nowhere else to go.

In one way or another, most of these answers describe a pigpen moment. Too often, we wait until things are falling apart to finally open our eyes. But God can use a desperate moment.

How do we reach these desperate moments? Usually by one of two ways:

1. Difficult circumstances
2. Deserved consequences

The Prodigal Son experienced both of them.

Difficult Circumstances

Remember that famine? There's never a good time for your entire country to run out of food, but the timing couldn't have been worse for the Prodigal Son. He hadn't done anything to cause the famine. He had no control over it. It wasn't his fault.

Like me, most of you reading this have no idea what starvation feels like. But Jesus's audience would have known the horrors of a famine all too well. The Bible tells about one famine in Samaria that was so devastating people would buy dove dung to eat. Two mothers were so desperate they agreed to cook and eat their own babies.

But it was only when things got really hard that the Prodigal Son finally had a spiritual awakening. I've heard enough AHA stories to know that this is the usual chain of events. None of us would choose to go through tough times. But if we're honest, most of us have to admit that our AHA moments have usually come in the middle of difficult circumstances.

Erasing Famines

I read about a fascinating experiment psychologist Jonathan Haidt did. He handed the experiment's participants a brief summary of a person's life that looked something like this:

> Jillian will be born in August. As she grows, Jillian will develop a learning disability that will prevent her from learning to read at the appropriate age. Due to this disability, she will struggle with school for the rest of her years as a student. Despite her best efforts, her grades will always be average. In high school, Jillian will become best friends with a

girl named Megan. They will share secrets and be nearly inseparable for much of their junior year. But Megan will be diagnosed with a rare, aggressive form of cancer, and she will pass away just as senior year begins. Jillian will mourn the loss, and her grades will suffer for it.

She will attend a local community college, working a job and taking a small course load. The two-year program will take her three and a half years to complete, and just before heading to a state school, Jillian will be involved in a drunk-driving accident. A drunk driver will hit her from behind, pushing her car into an intersection, where a family of three will swerve to avoid her. They will skid off the road, hit a tree, and their youngest son will die. Though the fault isn't hers, Jillian will blame herself for his death and spiral into a deep depression.

Eventually, she will make it to a state school, finish her degree, and get a job working for a food distributor. She will love her job. Just as a promotion comes her way, an economic downturn will force the company to lay off much of their management, which now includes Jillian. In the devastated economic climate, Jillian will struggle to get work, and eventually she will file for bankruptcy, selling her house and moving into a small studio apartment to make ends meet. Though she will strive to get back on her feet, the economy will make it increasingly hard to do so, and she'll spend a few years living month to month.

She will eventually find another job, but due to her bankruptcy and season of unemployment, she won't be able to retire the way she thought she would, nor will she ever make as much as she used to. She will have to work hard into her old age, piecing her life back together.[2]

Here's the next part of the exercise: participants were asked to imagine that Jillian was their daughter, not yet born. This will be her unavoidable life story, but it hasn't happened yet. They had five minutes to edit her story however they wanted before she entered the world. With an eraser, they could eliminate whatever they wanted out of her life.

If you were a participant, what would you erase first?

Most of us would frantically erase the learning disability and the car accident and the financial challenges. Out of love, we would want Jillian to live a life without those hardships, pains, and setbacks. We all prefer lives free from pain and anguish—for ourselves, our friends, and our families.

But is that really what's best? I mean, do we really think a privileged life of smooth sailing is going to make us happy? What if you erase a hardship that's going to show Jillian how to be joyful despite any circumstance? What if you erase some pain that ends up being

2. John Ortberg. "Don't Waste a Crisis," *Leadership Journal, Christianity Today Library,* January 31, 2011, www.ctlibrary.com/le/2011/winter/dontwastecrisis.html.

the thing God uses most in her life? What if you erase a difficult circumstance that would wake her up to God's purpose for her life?

This may sound harsh, but the number-one contributor to spiritual growth is not worship, preaching, small groups, videos, or books. The number-one contributor to spiritual growth is … difficult circumstances. I've seen it in personal experience. I've seen it in research surveys. I've seen it in talking to thousands of people over the years. AHA comes out of the suffering, setbacks, and life challenges. Many people can point to those moments as their greatest moments of spiritual awakening.

My friend Lori lost her seventeen-year-old daughter in a tragic car accident. Six weeks later, her son was deployed to Iraq. Trust me—no parent is ever prepared to lose a child. But then to face the overwhelming fear of losing another child who was going off to fight a war … This was Lori's worst nightmare. What made things even worse was the fact that Lori and her husband had been separated for the past year. She felt utterly alone.

In this desperate moment, Lori realized that the only One who could hear her heart was God. She felt as though she had nowhere else to go, so she went back to church. That first weekend in church, she worshipped God with tears streaming down her face. Before her world had come crashing down, she didn't have much time for God. Now, in desperation, she began crying out to Him every day.

There are still tears when Lori tells her story, but they are tears of relief as she tells about God's power. He has given her a new sense of purpose. Lori and her husband recommitted their lives to Jesus and to each other. Her son recently returned from Iraq and got married.

All that pain and loss and fear was the worst part of Lori's life. But now she looks back and sees incredible spiritual awakening. The Bible says, "Sometimes it takes a painful experience to make us change our ways" (Prov. 20:30 GNT). It's true. Sometimes it takes cancer to awaken us to the value of what's eternal. Sometimes it takes a car crash to jolt us to deeper prayer. Sometimes it takes a broken heart for us to finally let Jesus in.

Which Way Will We Go?

AHA isn't automatic. Difficult circumstances don't always wake us up. Sometimes we still roll over, cover our head with our pillow, and go back to sleep. Disappointment in life usually brings one of two opposite responses: either we cry out to God in desperation, or we turn and walk away from God. We blame Him. "God isn't holding up His end of the deal," we say. "Look at the hand I've been dealt. It's not fair! This isn't the way my life is supposed to go. If God isn't going to be there for me, then I'm not going to be there for Him."

Remember Job[3] in the Bible? Job was living the good life. He had a big family. He owned thousands of animals—serious status back then. He was rich, and he was a good man. The Bible says he was blameless and pure and a great man of God (Job 1:8).

But Satan said difficult circumstances would make Job turn his back on God. "Take away everything he has—he will curse you to your face!" Satan said. And God replied, "All right, you can try it."

---

3. That's *Job* as in rhymes with *robe*—not *job* like the work you get paid to do.

From there, Job's life blew up. A storm destroyed a house, which then crushed his kids. A skin disease broke out all over his body. He lost his animals, his wealth, his children, his health—everything. His wife was done with him. She told Job, "Curse God and die!" (Job 2:9). Job pleaded with God: "What have I done to deserve this?" But in the middle of all the pain, Job experienced an awakening. It was his AHA moment.

"My ears had heard of you but now my eyes have seen you," he said (Job 42:5).

In his pain, Job saw God more clearly. The alarm sounded, and his eyes were opened. In his disappointment he didn't distance himself from God; instead he moved closer.

I know someone reading this right now has experienced or is going through some difficult circumstances. In all your pain and disappointment, there's part of you that wants to turn from God and walk away. But don't waste the pain. Hear the alarm and wake up. "God sometimes uses sorrow in our lives to help us turn away from sin and seek eternal life," the Bible says (2 Cor. 7:10 TLB). It doesn't say *causes*; it says *uses*. Pain and problems happen on their own in this broken world. But God wants to use the difficult circumstances to draw you closer to Him.

I caught part of a radio interview with a guy named Gerald Sittser. He's a professor at Whitworth University in Spokane, Washington. Years ago a drunk driver hit Gerald's minivan. In that accident, he lost three generations. He lost his mom, his wife, and his young daughter. Gerald somehow walked away without physical injury. In the interview I heard, he talked about what it was like to experience that kind of loss. Eventually Gerald wrote a book called

A Grace Disguised in which he described his difficult journey. And here is what he concluded: "The experience of loss does not need to be the defining moment of our story." He went on to say that *our response* can be the defining moment of the loss.

When difficult circumstances come your way, how will you respond? When famine hits your land—when pain hits your life— how will you respond to it? If you let Him, God will use those circumstances to wake you up and draw you closer to Him. Your story can be about much more than loss.

Deserved Consequences

The other kind of consequences are the ones we bring on ourselves. Jesus pointed out in the parable of the prodigal son that he "squandered his wealth in wild living" (Luke 15:13). That's no one else's fault.

When the son arrived in the distant country, he lived it up. Night after night, he was the life of the party, buying round after round. But before long, he was left with an empty glass and an empty wallet. The money was gone, and there was no one to blame but himself. His own actions and choices brought consequences. He ended up in a pigpen, where he was so hungry he drooled over the pigs' food. If he hadn't left his father's house and blown all his money partying, he wouldn't have been in this position.

The consequences of our choices can be a jarring alarm that shakes us awake in a hurry. When you're in the Distant Country, it's only a matter of time until your decisions catch up to you. That desperate moment is the time to cry out to God.

A few months ago, I was speaking at a church in Las Vegas. It was Sunday morning, and I was driving to the church when I got pulled over for "drunk driving." There is a reason I put those words in quotes. I wasn't drunk. However, I had made some poor choices that led up to this moment.

Poor Choice #1: When I got off the plane and headed to the car-rental counter, I decided I was going to try to charm my way into getting upgraded to a convertible—which turned out to be pretty easy. It was 114 degrees outside, and every single convertible they had was available. So I was driving in a canary-yellow Mustang convertible with the top down early on a Sunday morning.

Poor Choice #2: I wasn't supposed to be staying on the Strip, but because I wanted to be close to the action, I got a room at a Holiday Inn right behind a casino. So it looked like I was pulling out of a casino, driving a convertible with its top down early on a Sunday morning.

Poor Choice #3: I was running a little bit late that morning, so I left my room looking a little disheveled. I say a little disheveled, but honestly, I looked like a mess with my shirt untucked, my hair gloriously, bed-headedly askew, and my pants more wrinkled than normal. At the time, I didn't think much of it. I figured I'd be able to touch up my hair and make myself look presentable after I arrived at the church. So it looked like I was pulling out of a casino, driving a convertible early on a Sunday morning, and I happened to look like the victim of an all-night bender.

Poor Choice #4: I had run into a gas station the night before to get some gum and made a last-minute decision to splurge on IBC

Root Beer. I love IBC Root Beer, but my wife's not a big fan because it's more expensive since it comes in a glass bottle. A little was left over, and I decided to finish off the bottle as I drove with messed-up hair and wrinkled clothes out of a casino in a convertible with its top down early on Sunday morning.

Poor Choice #5: When the police officer pulled me over for drunk driving, the situation struck me not just as humorous, but as hilarious. I started laughing and couldn't stop, which I am known to do in completely inappropriate situations.[4] This frustrated the officer, who explained to me that this was not a laughing matter. As I tried to stop laughing, I explained to him that I wasn't drunk but on my way to go preach at a church.

To which he responded, "That's exactly what a drunk person would say."

As he walked back to his car, my laughter devolved into soft chuckling.

When he got back into his car, I was only smiling.

Once he got on the radio with my license in hand, I started waking up to reality.

I retraced my steps, and my five poor choices became evident. I suddenly got this sick feeling in my stomach—the emotional equivalent of eating a bean burrito in less than ninety seconds. I realized that all of this had gone horribly wrong, and it could get much worse. So while I was waiting for the police officer in my canary-yellow

---

4. For example: when my wife was pregnant with our first child and we went to the hospital for birthing classes, they showed us a video of women in labor. I couldn't stop laughing. My wife failed to see the humor.

convertible, do you know what I started doing? I prayed—and with great fervor, I might add.

Wake Up

The moment the consequences for our decisions catch up to us is an invitation to cry out to God for help. There's a prophet in the Bible who experienced this moment. His name was Jonah.

If you've seen only the VeggieTales version of this story, there's a little more you should know. It began with God giving Jonah an assignment to go preach in Nineveh. Nineveh wasn't exactly an Israelite tourist hot spot. It was a mighty city in Assyria, a world power at the time. People were afraid of the Assyrians. Assyrians didn't just conquer a nation; they practiced genocide. If their enemies survived, they tortured them. They were very good at what they did.

Is it any surprise that this was the last place Jonah wanted to go? So he decided to take a boat to Tarshish, which was in the exact opposite direction as Nineveh. He ran from God, heading to the Distant Country.

Jonah was on the ship heading to Tarshish when a violent storm struck. Now if I'm on a boat, any storm is a bad storm. But a storm sent by God? It was so bad the sailors were terrified. The sailors cried out to their gods and gave up any hope of overcoming the storm themselves. That's like the captain of an airplane getting on the intercom and saying, "This weather's really bad, folks. I've lost control of the plane, and I'm really scared right now. Would everybody please start praying? By the way, I'm about to open the cargo hold and let all our luggage plummet to the ground."

That's what the captain of this ship did. While the crew was throwing all of the ship's cargo overboard, he found Jonah belowdecks. Amazingly, Jonah was sleeping! Even the captain couldn't believe it. The pagan captain shook Jonah awake and said, "Come on, man— pray! Whoever your god is, maybe He'll listen and help us!"

Jonah had run from God. And there were consequences— deserved consequences. Now he was dozing through the alarm God had sent. Everyone else was extremely aware of the disaster at hand, but Jonah was oblivious. He was in desperate need of a sudden awakening.

And this is where some of you find yourselves. You are sleeping through the storm. Everyone around you can see it, but you are snoring in the face of disaster. You need someone to wake you up.

As a pastor, I've often had to run belowdecks to wake up someone who was sleeping through a life storm. So let me play the part of the captain for a moment, because you may be reading this and desperately need to wake up to call upon God.

To the one whose academic career is falling apart but who seems too distracted by video games to notice. *Wake up!*

To the student who's in the habit of getting drunk and sleeping with strangers. *Wake up!*

To the college freshman whose Bible has gotten buried in dust or lost in a closet. *Wake up!*

I am pleading with you to come to your senses. There's a storm brewing, and there is no time to waste. Don't fool yourself into thinking that those closest to you will be able to escape the devastation of your storm. Your journey to the Distant Country doesn't affect just you; it affects all those who share life with you.

When Jonah ran from God, the sailors were terrified. Their lives were at risk. Jonah's running led to the near destruction of the people around him. So it's not just me yelling at you to wake up. It's a friend, a boyfriend or girlfriend, a teacher yelling, "Wake up!" It's the voice of a parent shouting, "Honey, wake up!"

Desperation Reveals Dependence

Our desperate moments often reveal our total dependence on the Father. It was already true that we completely needed God. That was reality. But it may take a moment of desperation for us to realize it.

The Prodigal Son got desperate after he ran out of money and was forced to work in a pigpen during a famine. He realized he'd been dependent on his father his whole life—and still was. Think about it: He grew up in his father's house. He ate food from his father's fields. He wore clothes his father paid for. He drank and washed with water from his father's well. And when he wanted to head out on his own, where did he turn for the funding? His father! Even when he rebelled, he was dependent on his father! In the distant country, he lived and partied off the inheritance from his father. Finally, the Prodigal Son became desperate only when he ran out of his father's money.

The question is: How desperate will you have to be before realizing your dependence? Eventually, the money will run out or the famine will come.

The principal will call you in, sit you down, and say, "I'm sorry. You're out of chances."

Your boyfriend will say, "It's over."

Your parents will sit you down and ask about the sites in your laptop's Internet history.

The phone will ring, letting you know there has been an accident.

There will be a desperate moment, maybe a difficult circumstance, maybe a deserved consequence. One way or another, you will realize that your way isn't working and you need your heavenly Father.

What's It Going to Take?

Sometimes I speak to a group of inmates at the Kentucky State Penitentiary. They file into the room with no pretense or pride. They're all dressed alike. It's hard to get caught up in impressing people when everyone wears the same outfit—which declares their guilt. The inmates could teach the church a lot about authenticity and transparency.

Last time I was there, I talked about the Prodigal Son and how he had a moment of awakening. Afterward one of the inmates came up and showed me a picture of his family, which he kept in his Bible. As he looked at the image of his wife and two young kids, his eyes welled up with tears. "I tried it my way for a long time, and it didn't work, so now I'm doing things His way," he said. I put my arm around him and told him I was proud of him. But as he stared at his picture, he added, "I just wish it hadn't taken being sent here for me to come to my senses."

Over the years I've noticed there's something people often say after they come to their senses and return home from the Distant Country: "I had to hit rock bottom." Have you ever heard that? I don't know why we tell ourselves we have to hit rock bottom. I suppose it makes us feel better about how far we fell. But listen, you don't have to hit rock bottom. You can wake up now. You can come to your senses now.

Chapter 4

A STARTLING REALIZATION

There were these pictures, called Magic Eye, that were really popular in the mid-'90s. If you looked at them just right, you could see a hidden picture. You'd stare and stare, and then suddenly, when your eyes glazed over the right way, a 3-D image was supposed to appear. Maybe you saw one when you were a kid. For a while, these pictures were everywhere. People loved them!

But I hated them. I could never see the image.

A neighborhood friend of mine named Terry Good had one hanging on his wall. Whenever I went to his house, I'd stare at that picture until it felt like my eyes were bleeding.

"Do you see it? Do you see it now?" he'd ask. "How about now? Do you see it now?"

And I'd be like, "See what? I don't see anything."

Then he'd tell me something like, "You have to really *want* to see it."

Well, what was I supposed to do? I was staring a hole through this picture and still didn't see anything. Terry tried to help me with this piece of advice: "Whatever you do, don't blink." Have you ever tried not to blink? The harder you try not to blink, the more likely it is to happen. Seriously. Put the book down right now, stare at something, and repeatedly tell yourself not to blink.

The whole situation was frustrating. It was exasperating. And eventually I decided it was either a practical joke or Terry was smoking something. But then one day—after fighting the instinct to blink for twenty-seven minutes—I suddenly saw it! It was a sailboat floating among the clouds. And do you know what my response was? Massive disappointment.

But here's the point: For a long time I was staring at the picture right in front of me, and I couldn't see it. Then suddenly I saw it.

Have you had that kind of sudden awakening? The kind when you see something right there in front of you that you'd somehow been missing for who knows how long?

That's the way it was when the Prodigal Son came to his senses in the pigpen. Suddenly he realized, *It doesn't have to be like this.* He said, "How many of my father's hired servants have food to spare, and here I am starving to death!" (Luke 15:17).

Have you ever had a moment like that? You may not have realized it at the time, but the Holy Spirit opened your eyes, and you saw something you'd somehow missed before. You had a startling realization that changed everything.

I was talking to a guy whose life had been an ongoing struggle with alcoholism. He had tried to make changes many times. He went through the twelve-step program, which helped for a while, but he was never really on the wagon long enough to fall off. Over the years he realized how much his drinking had cost him. But even when he thought he had finally hit rock bottom, things fell even further.

Then one day he was listening to a sermon, and the preacher talked about the Bible verse in which Paul said, "Do not get drunk on wine, which leads to debauchery. Instead, be filled with the Spirit" (Eph. 5:18). Immediately this truth from God's Word opened his eyes. He came to his senses with this startling realization: He had been looking to alcohol to do for him what the Holy Spirit was meant to do. When he was depressed, he would drink for some comfort and peace, but the Holy Spirit wanted to comfort him. When he was feeling insecure, he would drink to feel a sense of security and boldness, but the Holy Spirit wanted to fill him with courage and strength. When he was uncertain about the future and what he should do next, he would drink to help him cope, but the Holy Spirit wanted to guide and direct him. The startling realization of that truth is what he needed to finally change.

Jesus put it this way: "The truth will set you free" (John 8:32).

Have you had some moments like this with the truth? You realize something you have never realized before, and it wakes you up.

You realize you've been trying to live a Christian life through your own power and strength rather than through the power of the Holy Spirit.

You realize you weren't actually following Jesus—you were just following a list of rules.

You realize the reason you struggle with food is because you are trying to satisfy your soul by filling your stomach.

You realize you cut because you're trying to keep your pain instead of letting God take it from you.

You realize you expect your dating relationship to make you happy because you've been looking to your boyfriend or girlfriend to do what only God can do for you.

You realize you are stressed out about grades because you're putting your trust in your own abilities instead of in God.

Suddenly you realize a truth. The truth has always been true, but for some reason you just haven't seen it. Suddenly it is the right time and the right place. And like the Prodigal Son, you have a startling realization that wakes you up and brings you to your senses.

Silence and Solitude

The Prodigal Son must have had some time alone to finally make his startling realization. He must have had some time to think. My guess is that it was the first time in a long time that he'd sat in silence. It wasn't his choice. It was just his reality. He'd run out of money. His friends had bailed on him. Famine swept the land. And he was driven to a pigpen.

It sounds like a scene from an old Western movie—the scene right before a gunfight. *Whoosh!* Everyone's gone. There's nothing left but tumbleweeds. For the Prodigal Son, there was no one to talk to. There was nothing to do. The parties were over. The crowd was gone. The son was now alone in the distant country. The only wild living was with the pigs. No more staying up all night and sleeping in late with no time for sober thinking.

If you're in need of a startling realization in your life, solitude and silence are where to begin. You may find that God has been trying to get your attention for a while, but you haven't been able to hear Him. Not because He hasn't been loud enough, but because you haven't been quiet enough.

It's like this: You're at home trying to watch a game or play a video game. You already have the TV turned up fairly loud, but you still can't hear what's going on. Why? There's too much noise in the house. Someone is using the blender in the kitchen. The vacuum cleaner is running in the living room. Your brother has his music cranked up down the hall. So you grab the remote and turn the TV volume up all the way. But you still can't hear. What's the problem? The problem isn't that you need to turn up the volume. The problem is that you need to turn down the noise. It's not that the TV isn't loud enough—it's that everything else is too loud.

God often speaks to us in solitude and silence. When we get away from all the noise and distraction, we tend to have a startling realization. The process usually plays out a little bit like it did for the prophet Elijah.

One of Elijah's AHA moments with God took place on a mountain. Elijah went to the mountain to meet with God, but when he got there, God hadn't shown up yet. While he was waiting, a strong wind blew through. Elijah thought, *Oh, God must be in that wind.* But the wind died down, and God wasn't there. Then an earthquake shook the whole mountain. *God must be in the earthquake,* Elijah thought. That would be how God gets our attention, right? But God wasn't in the earthquake. Next came a big fire. *Okay, God must be in the fire,* Elijah thought. Nope. No God. The catastrophic fireworks had come and gone without God's arrival.

Finally God spoke to Elijah … in the gentlest whisper you can imagine. The literal translation of the original Hebrew language describes a sound that's even quieter than a whisper—as the "sound of sheer silence" is how one Bible translation says it (1 Kings 19:12 NRSV). And that's how Elijah heard God.

For many of us, a little silence and solitude are the only things standing between us and a startling realization. But silence and solitude don't seem to be in our nature. When we find our lives falling apart in the Distant Country, we get desperate, and we want to make it happen ourselves.

A number of years ago, my youngest daughter was in the backyard, trying to catch butterflies. At this time of year, we had a bunch of butterflies staying in a certain area of our farm. From inside the house, I watched as she tried to grab a butterfly. She wanted one so badly she was working up a sweat thrashing around trying to grab hold of one. She wasn't trying to catch one so much as she was trying to seize one. Her arms flew around as she lunged toward one butterfly, then another. After watching her for a few minutes, I realized that the more frustrated she became, the more aggressive and forceful she was.

I finally went outside and explained how to catch a butterfly.

"Look," I said, "I know what I'm about to ask you is going to be really hard, but if you want to catch a butterfly, you need to be still and quiet. If you can just stand in the middle of them and be still and quiet, after a few moments, one of them will land on you."

She looked skeptical but was desperate enough to give it a shot. As I watched from a distance, she waited for one to land on her, and sure enough, after a few moments, one landed on her knee. And the moment that poor butterfly landed on her knee, she grabbed it.

Sometimes we want to seize AHA. But AHA can't be seized. It's received, and receiving it often requires a little silence and solitude.

So do you have any quiet moments in your life? Do you take the time to listen? Do you turn off your phone, tablet, iPod, PlayStation, TV, computer, or whatever other device that adds to the constant noise of your days? Do you pause from the social drama of who likes whom and who wore what and whose party is the place to be seen? Do you rest from the nonstop pace of assignments and classes and practices and clubs and applications and internships? Do you ever breathe deeply? Do you ever have quiet?

The songs of the Bible, the Psalms, say, "Be still." God says, "Be still, and know that I am God" (Ps. 46:10). I like this definition of stillness: silence on the outside and surrender on the inside.

I read about a church in England that recorded the "sound of silence" on a CD and provided the CD to the congregation with the challenge to listen to it once a day over the next week. It was marketed as a half hour of listening to absolutely nothing. What's crazy is that this church has been selling the CD to customers around the world.

You may not have a recording of the sound of silence readily available, but I would encourage you to get alone with your Bible and spend some time in solitude and silence anyway.

AHA often begins in the stillness.

Flip the Switch

A handyman came to our house to hang a light fixture in the kitchen because I was having a busy week. Well, that and the fact that I'm the least handy man you will ever meet.[1] So the handyman came over and got everything hooked up. He connected all the appropriate wires and then flipped the switch. Nothing happened. I was secretly delighted with his failure.

He rewired it. Then he turned it on again, but it still didn't work. He took everything down, disconnected the wires, and started over. But it *still* didn't work. My wife was starting to get a little frustrated, thinking the light she bought from the store was a dud. Meanwhile, I'd analyzed the situation and had become fairly certain that he wasn't flipping the right switch. He was flipping the switch next to the one I thought he should be flipping. But I wasn't going to say anything about my hypothesis for fear of being wrong and eliciting further mockery and humiliation for my lack of handyman skills. So I waited until he had it hooked up, and I walked over to the wall and flipped the switch. Immediately the light came on. *How do you like me now, Mr. Handyman?* It had been right there in front of him. He just needed someone else to flip the switch.

Sometimes the startling realization takes place only when someone else steps in with a healthy perspective and flips the switch for us. The Prodigal Son, and many of us, needs a little solitude and silence. But sometimes we also need someone else to tell us the truth we are having a hard time seeing.

In 2 Kings 5, the Bible tells a story about a guy who desperately needed someone to flip the switch for him. His name was Naaman,

---

1. True story: Growing up my dad taught me that the only two tools you needed to fix anything are a telephone and a checkbook. His toolbox consisted of a hammer and Super Glue.

and he was a successful and highly regarded military official for the king of Aram. The Bible describes him as a brave warrior. But Naaman's life started to fall apart when he discovered he had a horrible skin disease—leprosy.

Because Naaman had led a few raids on Israel, he had a young Israelite girl who served his wife. "If only my master could meet the prophet of Samaria, he would be healed of his skin disease," the girl said.

Naaman was desperate and willing to try any experimental treatment. So he got his king's blessing to go meet this prophet named Elisha. The king of Aram even sent a letter with Naaman to the king of Israel that read: "When you get this letter, you'll know that I've personally sent my servant Naaman to you; heal him of his skin disease." It was a kind of intimidation tactic.

Translation: "You better fix this guy—or else."

The king of Israel got the letter and panicked. He tore his clothes in anguish—they did that when they were really upset back in those days—and cried out, "Who does this guy think I am—God? I can't cure awful diseases!" To be fair to the king of Israel, this was a particularly unfair situation. The king of Aram was using Naaman's situation to create yet another excuse to raid Israel and make war against God's people.

But Elisha heard about it. "Don't worry," he told the king. "Send Naaman to me."

So Naaman made his way to see this prophet he'd heard so much about. He traveled a long way, and he didn't travel light. He brought 750 pounds of silver, 150 pounds of gold, and an entourage of horses, chariots, clothes, and supplies. Naaman came prepared to earn his healing, no matter what the prophet may order. A quest to the edge of Israel? Bring it on. A specific mountain he would need to climb or a people to conquer? No problem. A big payoff? Here you go. Naaman was ready for whatever the prophet would throw at him—except, of course, Elisha's curveball response. Second Kings 5:10 tells us, "Elisha sent a messenger to say to him, 'Go, wash yourself seven times in the Jordan, and your flesh will be restored and you will be cleansed.'"

Sounds simple enough, right? In practical terms, sure. But Elisha had insulted Naaman in every way possible. Naaman had arrived at Elisha's door with his caravan, and the prophet didn't even come out to greet him. Instead, Elisha sent a messenger. Naaman was not the kind of guy who received messengers. He *sent* messengers. So Namaan's pride was wounded twice over. He complained, "I thought that he would surely come out to me and stand and call on the name of the LORD his God, wave his hand over the spot and cure me of my leprosy" (2 Kings 5:11). Naaman had pictured things going down a certain way. He expected the prophet to display the same kind of pomp and circumstance that Naaman had in his arrival. But the rest was worse.

Washing in the Jordan might sound picturesque to us, but the Jordan was a lowly river as far as Naaman was concerned. Naaman stormed off in a huff. There was no way he was going to lower himself by taking a bath in an Israeli river. "I could have taken a bath in much better rivers back home!" he complained.

For Naaman, any scenario was better than the one Elisha had presented. So he sulked off in the dark, in desperate need of AHA.

At this point in the story, Naaman wasn't going to get healed unless there was a startling realization. He needed someone to flip the switch. But who? Elisha, the man of God? No. Maybe a fellow soldier in the caravan? Nope. Of all the people, it was a servant.

A lowly servant approached the pouting commander. "Um, sir? If the prophet had told you to do some great thing, you would have, right? So isn't it even easier to do what he says by washing in the river?"

This servant pointed out a simple truth. Naaman had come ready for an epic adventure or a grand healing ceremony. He was prepared to pay any price for his healing. So why not just wash? In the nicest way possible, the servant said, "Get over yourself and take a bath." The servant flipped the switch.

Naaman experienced a startling realization. Immediately, he went down to the Jordan and washed seven times. He was healed of his disease, and he returned to Elisha to express his awakening. "Now I know that there is no God in all the world except in Israel," he said (2 Kings 5:15).

AHA.

Do you have someone in your life who can flip a switch for you when it's needed? Do you have a friend who will do that? Have you given someone the permission and freedom to speak the truth to you even when it's not easy? Because we're often the last one to see the hard truth in our own lives. And we have a tendency, even in our close relationships, to speak only 95 percent of the truth. But it's that 5 percent that really needs to be said. That 5 percent holds the startling realization. We all need a friend who has permission to flip the switch that we missed.

Don't Stay in the Dark

I recently read an article in the *Montreal Gazette* about a man named
Pierre-Paul Thomas. He was born blind and could only imagine the
world that was often described to him. For years he walked with
a white cane to avoid obstacles in front of him. But at the age of
sixty-six, Thomas fell down the stairs in an apartment building and
fractured the bones of his face. He was rushed to the hospital with
severe swelling around his eyes. A team of doctors went to work to
repair the bones. Months later he went to be examined by a plastic
surgeon for a consultation about repairing his scalp. The surgeon
casually asked Thomas, "Oh, while we're at it, do you want us to fix
your eyes, too?"

Thomas did not understand. Nor did he know how to respond.

A couple years after that, Thomas had surgery and could truly
see for the first time. Suddenly his world consisted of bright colors he
had never fathomed before. He spoke of being awestruck by flowers
blossoming and trees blooming.

As beautiful as this story of a sixty-eight-year-old man who was
able to see for the first time is, there is a sad reality. He could have
had the same surgery at a younger age and been able to see earlier.
Thomas had assumed such a possibility was impossible and had
resigned himself to a life of blindness when, in reality, he could have
experienced the gift of sight decades earlier.[2]

---

2. Aaron Derfel, "Blind No More: 'It's Like I'm a Child All Over Again,'" *Montreal
   Gazette*, July 26, 2013, www.montrealgazette.com/health/Blind+more+like
   +child+over+again+video/8711875/story.html.

I don't want to spend any part of my life missing out on what God wants me to see. I don't want to come to my senses in twenty years if God is trying to wake me up now. Maybe it will take a desperate moment or a startling realization or a friend flipping the switch—but is God trying to get your attention?

Lord, open our eyes that we may see.

PART 2
BRUTAL HONESTY

He said to himself…

Chapter 5

TALKING TO YOURSELF

I was getting my hair cut at the barbershop[1] a few years ago, and I couldn't help but notice that the woman cutting my hair kept looking at me in the mirror. At first I didn't think much about it, but then her staring got more intense. Finally she stopped cutting my hair altogether and just stared at my reflection. Now I was looking at myself in the mirror, too, trying to figure out the problem. Maybe she cut one side a little too short and was trying balance it out? I gave my hair a once-over, and it seemed fine. But the woman kept staring, and her expression clearly said, "There's something wrong with you." Then she noticed that I was staring at her staring at me, and her expression changed slightly. She raised an eyebrow with a look that said, "Are you seeing what I'm seeing?" At this point, I was afraid to ask, so we both went back to staring at my reflection in the mirror.

---

1. I don't know why, but as a man I feel weird about calling it a salon. Maybe that's what it says on the front of the building, but I was getting my hair cut at the barbershop.

A few seconds later—and without a warning—she pulled on my right ear. "Don't you see it?" she asked. I didn't see it, so she tugged harder on my ear. But I was still oblivious. Whatever was so obvious to her was invisible to me. Finally she dropped the bomb: "Did you realize that your right ear sticks out farther from your head than your left ear?"

This was where everything clicked into slow motion. We were both staring at my ear. When she spoke, it was like I was listening to her words from underwater.

"Caaan youuuu seeeee iiiiit?" she asked, tugging my ear again. "Caaan youuuu? Iiiit's thiiiisss onnnnne."

Oh! My! Goodness! I thought. *She's right. I've woken up every morning, looked at myself in the mirror for thirtysome years, and never noticed it, but this complete stranger cutting my hair is spot-on. My right ear sticks out farther from my head than my left ear. How have I not seen this before?*

I tried to jolt out of my state of shock. She was still staring at me, almost measuring how far each ear protruded. I didn't know how to respond, but this cataclysmic discovery made me feel compelled to say something. "Well … is there … is there anything you can do about it—you know, to fix it?"

I'd been hoping she'd brought up this abnormality because she had a solution. Maybe she could make a few adjustments to my typical haircut, maybe layer each side a little differently to balance things out. "No," she said. "I think it's just one of those things you have to learn to live with."

Well, thanks, barbershop lady. Thanks a million. You've told me something I can never unknow. Now every single morning when I wake up, I'm going to be forced to look in the mirror and see that Dumbo ear sticking out and ask, "Why me?" And every night I'll fall asleep on my right side, hoping that my mutant ear will crease just a little during the night and that for a few hours in the morning, at least, I can be normal until it flops back out. And you can't do a single thing about it. Thanks, barbershop lady. Thanks a lot.

Honest Look in the Mirror

Have you ever learned something about yourself—or had someone tell you something—that completely changed things? You were awakened to some truth, and from then on, for forever, you could never unlearn or unhear it? AHA includes more than just an awakening; it requires honesty.

The second ingredient of AHA is brutal honesty. There's an important phrase in Jesus's story about the Prodigal Son:

> He said to himself …

There was no one else around. It was just the pigs and the son. And he had a startling awakening.

Sometimes the hardest conversation to have is the one you have with yourself. Before you can be honest with others, you have to be honest with yourself. And brutal honesty begins when we look in the mirror and speak the truth about what we see. AHA requires you to tell the truth to yourself about yourself. That's what the Prodigal Son did:

> He said to himself, "My father pays many men who
> work for him. They have all the food they want and

more than enough. I am about dead because I am
so hungry. I will get up and go to my father. I will
say to him, 'Father, I have sinned against heaven
and against you. I am not good enough to be called
your son. But may I be as one of the workmen you
pay to work?'" (Luke 15:17–19 NLV)

The son was finally honest with himself about what he deserved.
That kind of honesty is difficult. The hardest person in the world
to be honest with is the person in the mirror—and I don't mean
the woman cutting your hair. I mean you. It'd be nice if we could
have the awakening without the brutal honesty, but that's not how it
works. No one likes to wake up to the recognition of their failures.
No one wants to look in the mirror and say, "I've had an awful attitude. All I've done is complain and criticize everyone around me," or
"I go shopping and spend money I don't have to make me feel better
about the things in my life I can't control," or "I'm pretending to be
someone I'm not to impress the people around me, but the truth is
I'm a hypocrite."

But if we try to get away from honesty, we will short-circuit
any real change that AHA may bring. When there's recognition but
no repentance, AHA doesn't happen. The awakening must lead to
honesty.

Busted

There's a big difference between regret and repentance—the actual
turning away from our wrongs. Too often we have an awakening and

regret the way things have turned out—but we won't turn away from our part in it. We hate that someone found out. We regret that we've been caught. But we'd still rather deceive people and cover things up instead of fessing up to the truth.

We've gotten used to our politicians, athletes, business leaders, and celebrities getting caught in scandals. You know how it goes. The public figure is exposed. The scandalous story is everywhere. In the next day or two, the celebrity issues an official apology and commits to getting some kind of professional help.

There's a book called *The Art of the Public Grovel* that describes that very process. In it, the author describes the difference between an apology and a confession: "An apology is an expression of regret: *I am sorry*. A confession is an admission of fault: *I am sorry because I did wrong*."[2] Do you see the difference?

The author of another book, called *The Art of Confession*, says that an apology addresses the audience, but a confession implies an inner change of heart.[3]

As a pastor it's pretty common for me to talk to someone who has come to me to confess a sin or some kind of ongoing struggle. There are often tears as he or she admits the truth. I know it's a difficult and humbling thing to do, because I've been there as well. But one of the questions I've learned to ask is, "Are you confessing this to me because you got caught?" That is almost always the case.

His parents found a joint on the floorboard of the car.

---

2. Susan Wise Bauer, *The Art of the Public Grovel* (Princeton, NJ: Princeton University Press, 2008), 2.

3. Paul Wilkes, *The Art of Confession* (New York: Workman Publishing, 2012), 4–5.

He got expelled for showing up at school drunk.

The college grades were posted, and partying had obviously taken its toll.

A pregnancy test came back, and she wasn't sure who the father was.

His mom walked in and saw what he was looking at on the computer.

Those are pretty common causes for the confessions I hear. Getting caught doesn't mean the honesty is insincere. But it does make it more difficult to know if I am listening to regret or repentance.

Did you ever get caught with your hand in the cookie jar when you were little? Young kids haven't learned to be truly sneaky yet. So whether it was a real or figurative cookie jar, your parents probably caught you in the act of doing something wrong at some point. And you probably said, "I'm sorry." But was the apology honest? Were you sorry for swiping a cookie without permission, or were you sorry you got caught? A young kid is often just sorry he didn't have a better plan to heist the cookies.

Now that you're older, you can understand this: God sees everything. The Bible says, "Nothing in all creation is hidden from God's sight. Everything is uncovered and laid bare before the eyes of him to whom we must give account" (Heb. 4:13). So it's not really an issue of getting caught. The honesty we're talking about is more than an acknowledgment; it's a brokenness. You're not just mumbling "Sorry" to the person who caught you. Instead, in an honest moment when no one else is around, you're telling yourself the truth, deeply understanding how wrong you are, and turning your back on that wrong. That's the difference between regret and repentance.

So have you followed up an awakening by being brutally honest with yourself? Here's what I want you to do if you're reading this at home: Go into a bathroom and shut the door behind you. Look in the mirror and read these questions out loud. After each question, look at yourself in the mirror and speak the honest truth. Some of these questions won't apply to you, but I hope they will move you to ask some relevant, hard questions to yourself about yourself:

1. Did you spend more time this week on Facebook or in prayer?

2. When is the last time you told someone, "I love you"?

3. How have you helped someone in need in the last month? Be specific.

4. When was the last time you said to someone, "I was wrong. Please forgive me"?

5. What's on your smartphone? In your Internet history?

6. When was the last time you prayed with your friends? With your family?

7. What sin have you not confessed to God or anyone else?

8. When was the last time you sat with an open Bible?

9. Did you spend more money this month on eating out than on improving God's kingdom?

10. Who besides God knows about your secret sin?

So let me guess: you scanned through the questions and didn't take the time to actually go through the exercise. How do I know? Because I know that's what I would do if I were reading this book. I'd read through the challenge and think, *I get it. I understand the point the author is trying to make. What an insightful guy.* Then I would move on, letting myself off the hook once again.

Listen, I hope you will actually do the exercise. I'll even make a section break right here so you don't feel pressured to read on. There's something powerful about going into a quiet room, shutting the door, looking in the mirror, and speaking truth to yourself about yourself. Try it.

Honest with Others

I'll go ahead and tell you up front—you aren't going to like this next part. You'll probably even come up with some reasons why this next part doesn't really apply to you or why it isn't really necessary in your situation. But I'm telling you—AHA won't happen without it.

Brutal honesty begins with telling the truth to yourself about yourself. That's hard enough. But you must also tell the truth about yourself to someone else.

The Prodigal Son understood there was no way around it. After telling himself the truth about his situation and what he deserved, he realized he also needed to be honest with his father. He nailed it when he said, "I will set out and go back to my father and say to him: Father, I have sinned against heaven and against you" (Luke 15:18).

As we've already talked about in this chapter, most of us don't practice voluntary confession. If we can, we avoid being honest with ourselves. So confessing our wrongs or weaknesses to someone else—are you crazy? It seems like an act of self-sabotage.

Imagine you're speeding, doing eighty in a sixty-five-mile-per-hour zone. You look down and realize how fast you are going. So you slow down. There is an awakening, and you are honest with yourself. That's got to be enough, right? But imagine the next day you see a police officer. You go up to him and say, "Officer, I want you to know that yesterday I was going eighty miles per hour in a sixty-five-mile-per-hour zone." He might lock you up on suspicion of insanity. That's because we don't voluntarily confess to cheating on a test, getting high, losing our temper, or flirting behind our girlfriend's or boyfriend's back. We usually don't confess unless we're busted.

Our natural instinct is to hide our weaknesses and failures, especially when we feel like we have an image to maintain. I know some of you are reading this and thinking, *No way am I going to tell anyone else about my secrets. It would be so humiliating to share my mistakes with someone else.*

That's especially true if you feel like you're supposed to be "the good Christian kid." Believe me, I know how you feel. I know how sick in the gut I feel when I even think about telling someone I'm wrestling with issues. It's embarrassing. People expect pastors to be spiritual and holy, and it's easy to justify all the reasons why it's better to be seen as someone who's got it all figured out. But the problem is I don't. Not even close. And I have learned the hard way that unless I'm willing to be brutally honest with someone else, the AHA experience stalls out.

When you're going the wrong way, it's hard enough to admit to yourself. The last thing you want is to have someone else find out you're lost. I get that. But consider the alternative for a second. When we don't share our struggles with someone, what options do we have? Pretend we know where we're headed? That's never worked out well—at least, not for me.

Guys, have you ever been driving, and a friend, maybe one who's a girl, tells you you're going the wrong way? My wife has an annoyingly accurate sense of direction, so this is a familiar scenario for me.

One time during our first year of marriage, we were returning from a vacation in Branson, Missouri. I was taking the back roads, because I'm a man and there are few things I enjoy more than taking shortcuts.

"This isn't the right direction," my wife said. I dismissed it the first time, but when she repeated her concern, I got a little defensive. She kept commenting. I kept driving down wooded roads, annoyed that my wife had any doubts about my ability to get us home. But—and I've never actually told her this—after one too many turns, I realized she was right. I was lost. I kept driving confidently, not wanting her to know that, inside, I was praying I'd see a mailbox or tractor or anything that looked familiar. At that point, I'd had an awakening, but I refused to acknowledge the reality of my current situation. Here's the strategy I came up with—just some spur-of-the-moment male brilliance. *I'm going to wait until she falls asleep,* I thought. *Then I'll turn the car around.*

That's exactly what I did. I intentionally kept driving the wrong direction for another twenty minutes until she fell asleep. Then I turned the car around and sped home. When I pulled into the driveway, I woke her up and said, "See, honey, we're here. I told you I knew where I was going."

Am I the only one who does that? The only one who realizes I'm going the wrong direction, have the awakening, have the sudden recognition—but instead of being honest about it, say, "I'm just going to keep going"?

Get It Out

Here's your next assignment: it's time to be honest with someone else—maybe the person you offended or sinned against. The more you protest, the more likely it is that you need to sit down with that person and talk.

Beyond that difficult conversation, ask God to show you someone in your life with whom you can be brutally honest. The kind of person you are praying for should be

- a Christian who shares your values,
- honest,
- trustworthy,
- full of grace.

Most Christians understand the importance of being honest with ourselves and with God. The Bible tells us that when we confess our sins to God, He is faithful and forgives us (1 John 1:9). Jesus took on the punishment we deserve when He died on the cross. Because Jesus died for our sins, God forgives us when we confess them. So we tell ourselves we don't have to go any further than that. "If I'm honest with myself and with God, that's enough," we justify. But AHA requires more. The Bible also says, "Therefore confess your

sins to each other and pray for each other so that you may be healed"
(James 5:16).

When we're honest with God about our sins, He forgives us. But
when we are honest with other people, we find healing. What does
healing mean? For one, confessing our sin to another person holds us
accountable and helps us find the encouragement we need to break the
cycle of our struggle. When we take what we've kept in the dark and
drag it into the light, we find that it loses much of its power over us.

But the healing is literal, too. The psychology textbook *Coping
with Stress* talks about the healing power of confession. It says people
who keep secrets have more physical and mental complaints, greater
anxiety, depression, and physical problems such as back pain and
headaches. It even says, "The initial embarrassment of confessing is
frequently outweighed by the relief that comes with the verbalization
of the darker secretive aspects of the self."[4]

Back in the early church, this kind of honesty was very common.
Confession was a much more intentional part of worship. Sin wasn't
looked at as a personal issue where each believer needed to do business
with God on his or her own. Those early followers of Jesus understood that hidden sin destroyed the unity of the church and destroyed
people. People even fasted and prayed to repent of other people's sins.
Members made public confessions to the whole church. And they
couldn't take the Lord's Supper until there was evidence of change.

You may have heard of John Wesley, a famous preacher from the
1700s. He was passionate about confession and accountability in the

---

4. C. R. Snyder, *Coping with Stress* (New York: Oxford University Press, 2001),
200, 205.

church community. Before people became part of his church, they would be asked a series of questions to make sure they were committed to honesty with other people. Here are a few:

- Does any sin—inward or outward—have control over you?
- Do you desire to be told of your faults?
- Do you desire that we should tell you whatever we think, whatever we fear, whatever we hear about you?

Talk about brutal honesty! What would happen if church leaders asked everyone those questions today? But I think at the heart of those questions is a desire for honesty, which can be hardest when we're unwilling to admit we're wrong.

One of my favorite preachers of all time is a man named Fred Craddock. He is in his eighties now but is widely regarded as one of the most effective communicators of God's Word in the past century. I recently read an article about him on CNN's website entitled "A Preaching 'Genius' Faces His Toughest Convert."

The story was about Fred Craddock's father, Fred Craddock Sr. He was not a Christian and was often skeptical of faith and critical of the church. Whenever preachers who lived near his father would reach out to Fred's dad, he would say something like, "I know what the church wants. Another name; another pledge."

As his father grew older, he began to have more serious health problems. Fred went to visit him on his deathbed and learned that people from a local church had been visiting. They prayed, brought meals to the house, and sent cards and flowers. Slowly the heart of his father had softened.

Fred's dad could no longer speak, so when Fred sat next to his father in the hospital, his dad picked up a Kleenex box and scribbled a line from Shakespeare's *Hamlet*: "In this harsh world, draw your breath in pain to tell my story."

"What is your story, Daddy?" Fred asked.

His father's eyes filled with tears.

He wrote three brutally honest words: "I was wrong."[5]

---

5. John Blake, "A Preaching 'Genius' Faces His Toughest Convert," *CNN*, December 14, 2011, www.cnn.com/2011/11/27/us/craddock-profile/index.html.

Chapter 6

DENIAL—IF I IGNORE IT, MAYBE IT WILL GO AWAY

My wife and I recently watched one of those news-magazine shows that usually go like this:

1) Find the most disgusting thing people unknowingly encounter every day—say wood pulp in fast-food beef.
2) Make a half-hour exposé about it.

It might sound lame, but five minutes in, you're hooked, captured by the freak-out factor. In this particular episode, the reporter was visiting different hotels with a black light. When he walked into a room, the purple glow of his truth-saber would illuminate germs and hidden stains. They glowed bright neon on the bedspread, carpet, curtains, etc. It was pretty disgusting.

In one of the more disturbing scenes, the reporter waited in the lobby looking for a victim. He finally cornered a poor unsuspecting couple—probably enjoying a great vacation—and asked if he could do his black-light experiment in their room. At that point, my wife and I were talking to the TV:

"Don't do it! This is going to ruin your anniversary! Run away now!"

Sadly, the couple didn't heed our warnings. They agreed to take the crew up to their room.

The husband and wife made small talk in the elevator about the museums in town. They were on the brink of a scarring event, and they were oblivious. The TV crew didn't give them a clue. When they walked into the hotel room, everything looked pristine, as if room service had just been there. My wife and I were impressed by the cleanliness. Maybe this room could survive the test.

Then the lights went out. There was a moment of silence, the kind you'd expect in a movie theater right before the monster was revealed. The black light came on, and the stains were brought to light. Unbelievably, it was the worst room yet. Neon stains glowed everywhere, including a suspiciously huge one on the carpet. My wife and I groaned. The couple started to panic. The wife began to scream, "Turn that off! Turn that off! Turn that off!"

She rushed over and turned the lights back on herself. In an instant, everything looked normal again. She started to calm back down, laughing nervously. "That's better," she said.

But … ummm … here's the thing—*the stains were still there.*

No one could see them, but that didn't change the reality of their existence.

The word for this is *denial*. Denial is turning off the black light to make the stains disappear. You pretend like everything is okay even though everything is not okay.

Even if you've never taken a psychology course, you've probably heard of Sigmund Freud. He defined denial this way: denial is a defense mechanism in which a person is faced with a fact that is too uncomfortable to accept, so they reject it despite overwhelming evidence.

Denial is what we often choose instead of brutal honesty. It's when we keep trying to live in a false reality after we're confronted with some uncomfortable or inconvenient reality.

I read about another example of denial. Want to guess the number-one way people respond to getting a bill in the mail that they don't have the money to pay? You guessed it—they don't open it. The truth is too uncomfortable, so they just pretend like everything is okay.

Denial is the same reason young drivers drive twice the speed limit without wearing a seat belt or why smokers ignore the warning on cigarette packages as they inhale. "It won't happen to me," they tell themselves. They ignore the warning signs. The evidence may be there—it might even be overwhelming—but our response is, "Turn that off!"

David's Denial

There's some classic denial in the Bible, too. Look at King David. The guy had it all. Israel's armies were conquering neighboring peoples and laying siege to enemy fortresses. He was at the top of his game.

But it was during this season of success that David made some devastating mistakes and then chose denial instead of being honest about his secret sins.

It began one night when David was on the high roof of his palace. It was the custom of the day for women to bathe on their rooftops at certain hours of the night. As part of their ceremonial baths, they were to bathe only with water that had been naturally gathered. And of course, they weren't able to have hot water by turning the faucet knob to the letter H,[1] but water on the roof would have been kept warm by the sun.

You see where this is going. Did David know what he was going to see when he stepped out onto that roof? I think this was David's version of getting up in the night to flip through pay-per-view channels. On this particular night, David saw a woman taking a bath and said to his servant, "Find out who *that* is."

The servant already knew the answer. "She is Bathsheba," he told David. But he didn't stop there. My guess is he swallowed hard before he added, "She is Bathsheba … the *wife* of Uriah the Hittite" (2 Sam. 11:3). What he was really saying was, "David, uh, king, the woman you are lusting over is the wife of one of your most trusted soldiers, who is out fighting for you on the battlefield right now. That's who that is."

It seems to me that during this rooftop moment, God was waving a big red flag for David. He was using a servant to try to get David's attention. But David was looking elsewhere. The truth didn't

---

1. Since we have four women in our home who like to take long, hot showers, I have taught my son that the letter H stands for "Hope you like it cold."

get through. David invited Bathsheba to the palace and had an affair with her.

Sometime later, Bathsheba sent a three-word note that changed their lives forever: "I am pregnant" (2 Sam. 11:5). This should have been an awakening moment that brought David to a place of brutal honesty. Time to come clean and confess. But David was in full denial.

He came up with a plan to bring Bathsheba's husband back from the battlefield. *Uriah will sleep with his wife,* David thought. *Then he'll assume the baby is his own.* So David asked a few questions and sent Uriah home, expecting him to do what any husband would do after weeks away from his wife. But Uriah slept on his porch. *If my men can't sleep with their wives while they're at war, then neither can I,* he thought.

When David heard about this act of loyalty, it should have been a repentant moment. Seeing Uriah's integrity and honor should have caused David to be honest with himself. It was time to stop living in denial. It was time to do the hard thing and confess his sin. Instead, David went deeper into denial.

He told Uriah to stay another day, and this time he got Uriah drunk. *He's got to give in and go to bed with his wife now,* thought David. But Uriah didn't go home.

David got even more desperate.

Let's pull over for a second and acknowledge something. If David had known on the roof where this whole thing with Bathsheba would take him, he would have walked away, no questions asked. If he had known that inviting her to the palace would lead him to consider murdering a faithful, innocent soldier, David would have gone to bed alone. But this is how denial works. Denial might start with refusing to acknowledge a morally gray area, but denial will always ask you to ignore more and more. Nobody starts with Step Z. They start at Step A and move closer to Z one small compromising step at a time.

Anybody at the end of a painful, broken road will tell you so. Nobody starts with, "I want to end up in prison for killing someone because I broke into his house to steal money because I was desperate for drugs." They just say okay to the first high.

David found himself at Step Y, and instead of choosing honesty, he chose a cover-up. He sent Uriah back to war carrying his own death sentence. David's fear of being found out was greater than the guilt he felt for murdering an innocent man. That's what denial can do to us.

Uriah got killed, and David thought it was finally over. Now he could move on, and no one else had to know what he'd done.

We wish that's how life worked, don't we? If only ignoring the problem would make it go away. But many of us have learned the hard way that an unopened credit-card bill doesn't make problems go away. Instead, every day of denial only increases the balance that will eventually have to be paid. Denial leads you further than you ever imagined you would go.

Reality Check

Let's go back to the Prodigal Son. He was still in the pig slop. Definitely not part of his life plan. He'd grown up as a rich kid. He'd probably been pampered and protected. Never in a million years did he expect to be serving pigs and starving to death. But that's where he was when Jesus said, "He came to his senses ..."

We don't really know how long it took the son to wake up and smell reality. Maybe a few days? Maybe a few weeks? He landed this awful job, but he didn't change anything about himself. He got to the point of wanting to eat pig slop but still didn't make any changes. He stuck with the job for a while, despite the overwhelming evidence that things had gone terribly wrong. He kind of pretended that his life was working out decently. *I'll just feed pigs for a little while, and it'll be fine.*

What keeps a person in the pigpen? Denial. So even though you're feeding pigs, even though you've been kicked out of school, even though you can't say no to alcohol, even though you make yourself the same promise every night, even though you can't remember the last time you got on your knees and prayed—you keep living like everything is going to be okay.

Notice in the parable what the younger son was honest about: he was honest about where he was. He said, "Here I am starving to death!" (Luke 15:17).

Take a minute and look around. Where are you? What's the reality of your circumstances? Reality means the state of things as they actually exist. Not the state of how we wish things were. So what actually exists in your life right now? Are you desperate yet or on your way there? Be honest.

Here's what honesty might look like. Say you have this awakening that you're in trouble financially. (Use it as an example and pretend your parents won't bail you out.) Things have gotten bad. Changes should have been made a long time ago, but now the situation is desperate. You come to your senses when your credit cards won't let you spend any more and the power company cuts your electricity. You know you have a problem, but it's another thing to be honest about where you are. And that is the essential next step. To tell yourself the truth, you have to look at where you're spending money. That means acknowledging unnecessary and—*ahem*—stupid purchases: $2,000 boots; a custom Avengers paint job … seriously? It means going through all your debts and laying them on the table. It might be embarrassing. It might be painful. But it's essential.

This is where so many of us get stuck. We have an awakening moment, but we lack the courage to be brutally honest with ourselves about our current reality.

Three Tactics of Denial

Unfortunately, we can be really good at denial. Have you mastered any of these techniques?

Disagreement

Have you ever been in a discussion with someone who was simply wrong, but who still disagreed with you? The more you debated, the clearer it became that her opinion had nothing to do with facts and everything to do with what she *wanted* to be true. It's like the old saying: "Don't bother me with the facts; my mind's already made up."

A few years back, I was talking with a college student who had grown up in my church. He was home on break when I ran into him. I asked how his freshman year was going, and he asked if we could sit down and talk. Here's how he began the conversation: "Hey, I wanted to talk to you because over the last few months I have been studying the Bible and have come to the conclusion that sex before marriage is not a sin."

He was intelligent, and he had done his homework on some different cultural insights. I pointed out some Bible verses from Thessalonians and Hebrews about honoring marriage and the intimacy of marriage. We talked about some Greek words and some different meanings of sex and the oneness God had in mind for marriage.

After a while, he finally said, "Look, maybe that is what it meant for the people in that time, but a lot of things have changed. So the meaning of this has changed. I don't think what was true for them is true for us in our culture. It's just a cultural difference."

Even though this guy knew what was right, he wanted to justify his decision to disobey God by disagreeing about how to interpret the Bible. I finally said, "Look, I don't know you that well, and I don't know much about your life. But let me guess that you grew up being taught that sex outside of marriage was against God's will. Is that true?"

"Yeah, that's true," he said. "I grew up thinking it was a sin. But I don't believe that anymore."

"Okay, let me make one other guess," I said. "My guess is that you've gotten yourself a girlfriend—and that you're sleeping with your girlfriend. Is that true?"

Silence.

Then he said, "Yeah, but that doesn't have anything to do with this."

That's denial. We disagree with what's true and tell ourselves a lie because the lie is more convenient to believe.

There was a Renaissance philosopher named Blaise Pascal who captured this truth. He supposedly said, "People almost invariably arrive at their beliefs not on the basis of proof but on the basis of what they find attractive."

We're willing to lie to ourselves about our reality and about what we believe if it means we can have something that we want.

AHA won't happen until we have a moment of brutal honesty and tell ourselves the hard truth. It won't happen until we agree that we're wrong. The Bible calls that confession. You come to a place where you stop disagreeing with the truth and you honestly say, "Here I am …"

Defense

I have a friend who is a personal trainer. I try not to have friends like this, but somehow it happened. The truth is that even though we are friends, I find myself avoiding him during seasons when I've gotten out of shape.[2] I feel bad around him because I look at him and his cut arms and brick-wall build, and then I look down at my pudgy midsection and just hate life for a few seconds. But then I get a cookie-dough Blizzard and everything is okay.

It never fails. When I'm with him, I get this feeling that he's staring at my gut. "How's your diet and exercise routine going?" he asks. I'm sure he's asking out of genuine concern, but I still get defensive. "I don't know. How's your prayer life and Bible memorization going?" I ask.

---

2. Like the past nine years.

Of course I say this from a safe distance.

Defensiveness often reveals an area of our lives where we're in denial. But actually avoiding the truth is hard to do. So we turn to more covert operations. We defend ourselves by avoiding confrontations with the truth. There's no way I can measure up to my friend—but maybe I can avoid him.

Most of us avoid the personal trainers in our lives. We try to avoid the people and places that force us to be brutally honest. I've discovered that this is often why people stop coming to church. I'll talk to people who come back to church after being away from it for a period of months or years, and they'll usually say something like this:

"When I went to college, I started partying, and I guess it was about that time I stopped going to church ..."

"I started dating this guy, and it wasn't long after that I stopped going to church ..."

"I made these new friends. That's right about when I stopped coming to church ..."

I'm not even sure if most of these people realize the connection they're making. But you see it, right? They—and we—avoid people and places that will confront us with the truth about where we are.

Remember the hotel room stains? That's how we respond to stains in our lives. If the light of God's Word shines on them, they show up. "Oh, look at these stains," we have to say—but we don't want to see them. We don't want to deal with them. We defend ourselves by trying to stay away from God's light and pretending like everything is okay. We avoid honest moments because sometimes the truth hurts. But AHA won't happen until we stop defending ourselves.

Distraction

It's easier to live in denial about one part of our life if the other parts are busy and going well. That must have been true for King David. His personal life may have been falling apart, but things were going well professionally. The nation of Israel was experiencing some of its best days.

Today, distracting ourselves into denial might look like the girl with two million Facebook friends who runs every club and youth-group event but who hasn't opened her Bible in months.

Or maybe it's the guy who knows every TV show and movie reference but fails to notice that all of his friendships are becoming more and more shallow.

Okay, so that example hits home for me, because as you can tell, I've been known to be sucked into TV shows before. A show I also watch sometimes is *Kitchen Nightmares*. Have you ever seen it? A world-class chef steps into restaurants that are—you guessed it—living nightmares. Usually the restaurant is on the verge of going out of business even though it often looks great on the outside. What's wrong is the food; it's nasty. And that's a big problem for a restaurant. The restaurant owners have typically already had a sudden awakening because the business is in trouble, but what they need is some brutal honesty.

And the show's host, Chef Gordon Ramsay, is brutal. He usually orders a half-dozen dishes and, with great passion and clarity, explains how horrible each one is. It's painfully entertaining how he tries over and over to get the restaurant workers to realize they are in an Oh no! situation.

Often, the problem is that the restaurant owners are in denial about the quality of the food because they're distracted by so many other things. They're managing food orders, overseeing waitstaff, shaking hands with customers—basically doing anything but actually cooking the food. It takes about three-quarters of the show for them to finally be honest about reality.

That can be difficult and painful. But AHA often begins with an Oh no! moment.

David's Oh No! Moment

David lived in denial for a year. He was still a successful king, writing psalms and winning wars, but he hadn't truly acknowledged his sin. He'd tucked it away and tried to wall it off from reality. He wanted to act like his affair happened in another world or another life. He wasn't being honest. He wasn't feeling broken over it. God had given him time, but David hadn't confessed. So God sent the prophet Nathan to have a "Chef Ramsay moment" with David.

"David, a situation has come up," Nathan said. "There are two men in your kingdom. One man is wealthy and has all kinds of sheep, a great herd. But his neighbor is poor and has only one lamb. This lamb is like a child to the poor man because he has nothing else. The lamb eats the food off his table and sleeps at the foot of his bed. But David, here's what happened: The rich man, the one with all the sheep, he had a friend over, and they decided that for dinner, they really wanted a rack of lamb. Instead of killing one of his own sheep, the rich man went over to his poor neighbor's house and took that lamb. He stole it, barbecued it, and served it to his friend. What should we do here, David?"

David was furious. He demanded justice. This was wrong and had to be fixed!

Right then, Nathan stopped him and said:

"You are that man."

After all the cover-ups and a year of denial, David finally broke. He was finally honest with himself, with Nathan, and with God.

Confession is the cure for denial. If he could have, David would have preferred to skip this part of AHA. We all would. After we have the sudden awakening, we're ready to move on with our lives. But lasting change and true transformation require confession. The original Greek word for *confession* in the Bible's New Testament usually means "to acknowledge." It means defining reality for what it is. It means telling yourself the truth about yourself and about the reality of your situation.

We can still read King David's confession. Psalm 51 records his prayer. Through brokenness and tears, David finally told the truth to himself and to God. He even references the "stains" in his life, but his response was no longer to turn off the lights and pretend like everything was okay. In the psalm, he turns on the light, exposes his stains, and asks God to wash him clean. Here is the beginning of David's prayer:

> Have mercy on me, O God,
>   because of your unfailing love.
> Because of your great compassion,
>   blot out the stain of my sins.
> Wash me clean from my guilt.
>   Purify me from my sin.

For I recognize my rebellion;
>   it haunts me day and night.
Against you, and you alone, have I sinned;
>   I have done what is evil in your sight.
You will be proved right in what you say,
>   and your judgment against me is just.
For I was born a sinner—
>   yes, from the moment my mother conceived
>   me.
But you desire honesty from the womb,
>   teaching me wisdom even there.

Purify me from my sins, and I will be clean;
>   wash me, and I will be whiter than snow.
Oh, give me back my joy again;
>   you have broken me—
>   now let me rejoice.
Don't keep looking at my sins.
>   Remove the stain of my guilt. (Ps. 51:1–9 NLT)

Stop.

Before you go to the next chapter, read Psalm 51 again. But this time, instead of just reading David's words, *pray them.*

Chapter 7

PROJECTION—IT'S NOT MY FAULT, SO IT'S NOT MY RESPONSIBILITY

Have you noticed there are warning labels everywhere? They're on everything, and many are so obvious they're almost funny. Your cup says, "Caution: Coffee May Be Hot." Your fireplace logs say, "Caution: Risk of Fire." Your sleeping medication says, "Warning: May Cause Drowsiness." Duh. Isn't that the point?

Do you know why most of those warning labels exist? Because someone sued the company over it—or the company is trying to be extra sure no one *will* sue them. Someone burned their mouth or spilled hot coffee on themselves and then sued the restaurant. So now we're all told that the hot coffee we order might be, well, hot. Let's say it again: duh!

There's actually an antilawsuit organization in Michigan that keeps track of these ridiculous, commonsense-defying labels. It's one way to show the impact of frivolous lawsuits on businesses over the years. They have a lot of examples of unnecessary warnings and the descriptions of the lawsuits behind them. One example is a tractor with a warning label that says, "Caution: Avoid Death." Always good advice, right? But the reason for the warning is that someone died goofing around on a tractor and the family sued the company.

Another good one is the stroller with a warning label that says, "Warning: Remove Infant Before Folding Stroller for Storage." Wow, so some parent[1] absentmindedly folded up his toddler and sued the company for it. Because clearly that was the stroller company's fault.

There's a Batman costume that had a warning label that reads "Warning: Cape Does Not Enable User to Fly." First of all, everyone knows Batman doesn't fly. That's Superman. But some kid got on the top bunk and launched spread-eagle across the bedroom, probably breaking a femur in the process. Mom came running in and said, "Doesn't that costume have a warning label on it?!" Because the kid clearly would have read it had it been there.

After seeing the website, I couldn't help but notice warnings around my house. The worst one I found was in my garage. The warning label on my chain-saw paints a pretty grim picture. It says, "Do Not Attempt to Stop Chain with Hands."

Our society is expert in blaming others for our own stupid choices. Instead of being brutally honest with ourselves, most of us want to place the blame on someone else. The word for this is *projection*. Denial is refusing to admit the reality of an unpleasant fact, but

---

1. And by *parent*, they mean *dad*.

projection is admitting reality without taking responsibility. We just blame someone else.

Blame from the Beginning

The use of projection is as old as time. Go back to the beginning of the Bible, in Genesis, where we read about the first man and woman. Adam and Eve were living a beautiful life in the Father's house. They lived in a garden called Eden, which was full of beautiful trees that grew delicious fruit. God specifically and clearly told them what they were not permitted to do. He said, "You are free to eat from any tree in the garden; but you must not eat from the tree of the knowledge of good and evil, for when you eat from it you will certainly die" (Gen. 2:16–17).

But you remember what happened. The Devil came on the scene and did what he does best. He lied. He told Adam and Eve they were missing out by not eating that fruit. He said the only reason God told them not to eat it was because He didn't want them to be like Him.

Eve took the fruit and took a big bite. She told Adam it was delicious, and he took a bite. Later God asked, "Have you eaten from the tree that I commanded you not to eat from?" That caused a sudden awakening. So how did Adam respond? He said, "Yes, God. I confess that I broke Your command. I have sinned and not obeyed Your word. Here and now I take responsibility for my rebellion. I don't deserve it, but I humbly ask You for Your grace and mercy."

Okay, you know this story, and you know that's not exactly how it went. Adam really said, "The woman you put here with me—she gave me some fruit from the tree, and I ate it" (Gen. 3:12).

That's projection. Instead of being honest and confessing his sin, Adam said, "God, this isn't my fault. It's her fault."

My wife is a bit of a handywoman. When she's in a fix-it mood but needs ideas for a project, she'll watch the DIY Network. I don't watch this with her very often, but it is entertaining to watch people who are less competent than I am, so I do find it somewhat amusing.

I especially get a kick out of a show called *Renovation Realities*. Each episode focuses on a couple that decides to take on a remodeling project. Like most reality shows, it's predictable. But the entertainment comes from watching the inevitable train wreck. The couples clearly don't watch the show—if they had seen even one episode, they would know that no couple has ever escaped a renovation unscathed.

Here's how it starts.

The couple kisses and high-fives. Then they dive into a rebuilding project together. They're excited. Things start off well. They pull down cabinets and make quick work of the ugly plywood. Encouraging words fill the air, and their optimism is contagious. Cue nondescript celebratory music. But by the commercial break it all goes wrong. The new wood they bought isn't the right color, and they've already damaged it. The wife will say something like, "I knew this was a bad idea." But she didn't. The husband will say something like, "I've got this under control." But he doesn't. It's a big mess. The new cabinets look awful, and they're not level. So the wife begins to blame the husband for his poor measurements. The husband blames the wife for ordering the wrong size as he *obviously* measured correctly!

That was Adam's approach too. There was only one other person on the planet with him, and Adam blamed her. And he blamed God, because God created Eve. After confronting Adam, God confronted Eve. She responded the same way as Adam. She blamed the serpent.

Instead of being brutally honest when they were confronted with the truth, Adam and Eve pointed fingers and blamed someone or something else.

The Blame Game

Projection is more than what happens on video screens. Projection is when we follow our sudden awakening with excuses and justifications. Instead of accepting responsibility, we assign blame:

I know it was wrong to change the numbers, but my teacher has unrealistic expectations.

I know it was wrong to plagiarize my paper, but everyone does it.

I was wrong to lose my temper, but you should see the rest of my family.

I was wrong to be disrespectful to my mom, but she just doesn't get it.

I know it's wrong for me to look at that stuff, but he sent it to me.

I know it was wrong to call her that, but she posted that mean comment.

The Prodigal Son could have projected like that. But he finally was honest about his reality and came out of denial when he recognized and agreed, "Here I am starving to death!" That's a big step, an important step. But so is what comes next. He could've said, "Here I am starving to death, but he …"

The son could have taken on the role of the victim and said, "It's not my fault." He could have pointed the finger at someone else.

There are other people in the Prodigal Son's story, and he could have chosen to use them in the blame game.

Think about it: the son could have blamed his friends. When he got to the distant country, he didn't spend all his money alone. He was the life of the party. It takes people to have a party. It's safe to assume that he blew all that money buying drinks for his new friends. But it seems that when the money disappeared, so did they.

Or how about the farmer? The son could have complained that he wasn't being treated fairly. Whatever happened to a fair day's wage? The farmer wouldn't even let the son satisfy his appetite with the pigs' food.

There were other options for the son to blame as well. Let's look at the two most likely targets for his projection—because they're ours, too.

The Father

Now we're getting deep. Don't you think the son could have blamed his dad for being too permissive or too passive? I mean, what kind of father just gives his kid an inheritance when it's asked for? If the son grew up in a home where everything came easily and his father never said no, it's no wonder he ended up starving in a pigpen, right?

Mom and dad are easy targets when it comes to projection. Instead of taking responsibility, many people blame their parents for the way they were raised—or are being raised. And sometimes it only seems fair.

We blame our parents for all kinds of things. When I was a kid my parents got us chocolate bunnies for Easter. Did you get chocolate bunnies? Every year I specifically remember hoping, *Maybe this*

Easter my parents will spend the extra money and get the solid chocolate bunny. But every year ended in disappointment. Every year the bunny was hollow. My dad would try to spiritualize the moment. "Yes, son, it's hollow on the inside," he'd say. "It's empty, just like the tomb on that first Easter morning." So I learned as a child to equate the resurrection of Christ with bitterness and disappointment. Thanks, Dad.

Okay, that's probably a little harsh. But it's easy to trace a lot of our bad decisions and difficult situations back to a mom or dad who just didn't get it right.

I listen for this when I talk to people who need to make a change in their lives. I listened to one single mom who had no trouble being honest about her reality. She'd been in and out of relationships her whole life. The longest she ever held the same job was eighteen months. She was buried under credit-card debt because she shopped to treat her depression. She admitted all this. But after defining reality for five minutes, she spent about fifteen minutes blaming her parents.

"What am I supposed to do? I can't change my childhood, can I?" she asked me. She went on to tell about parents who divorced when she was young. She didn't see her father much after that. Her mom had guys in and out of the house. Her dad remarried and started a new life. On the rare occasions she would visit his new family, she never felt like she was part of it. There were even times when she would be asked to take the picture of her dad and his new family but wasn't included in the actual picture.

It wasn't hard to sympathize with her. The truth is her parents did a lot of things wrong and deeply wounded her when she was young and vulnerable. But did her parents rack up the credit-card debt? Did her parents make her quit a dozen jobs? Did her parents decide whom she was going to date and break up with? She was being only partly honest with herself, and she was stuck in the pigpen of projection. As long as she continues to say, "It's not my fault," and blames her parents, AHA won't happen for her.

Lots of times, it seems so much easier to blame someone else, especially our parents. Imagine that every day you take lunch to school, and every day it's the same thing: chicken salad sandwiches. You continually complain to your friends that it's always chicken salad sandwiches in your lunch. You are so sick and tired of chicken salad sandwiches. You tell a friend you'd rather die than eat one more chicken salad sandwich. Finally somebody asks, "Why don't you ask your mom to make you something else?" And you reply, "Oh, actually I make lunch myself."

That's the reality for many of us. We end up in the Distant Country living in very difficult circumstances, and we make it sound like it's someone else's fault. But in reality, we are the ones making the chicken salad sandwiches each morning.

God

God is an easy target too. The son could have pointed at God for the famine or blamed Him for not being able to find a decent job. God rarely gets credit when things are going well, but He often gets the blame when times are tough.

A few years ago, I pulled into a crowded parking lot. After maneuvering through the aisles, I finally found a spot. It didn't matter that it was a compact car spot; I was going to park my truck there. I squeezed into the spot, sighing with relief. Looking at the sky, I realized I needed to get in and get home pretty quick. Ominous storm clouds were swirling overhead, the wind was picking up, and I did not want to be stuck on the road when the rain was unleashed. As a general rule, I find it's better for my spiritual well-being if I don't drive during torrential rain. Slick roads and stupid drivers bring out the worst in me.

So I was ready to dash into the store. I started to get out of the truck, and as I opened the door, the wind literally ripped it out of my hands. I watched my truck door slam into the new-looking Toyota Camry next to me. I left my insurance information for the owner of the car, thinking I would have to pay for the damages.

A few days later, I was on the phone with my insurance agent explaining what happened. And he said something that shocked me. "Well, this isn't your fault," he said. I told him there was no way it was the other guy's fault because he was in the store at the time.

"No, it's not your fault because this is what we call an act of God," he said.

I was like, "Really, this is God's fault? We can blame Him for this?" And it turns out that *act of God* is a legal term. So instead of taking responsibility for parking too close or not hanging on to the door tightly enough, I got to blame God.

That's what many of us do. If our relationships don't meet our expectations, if we fail a class, if our moms ors dad let us down, if the college doesn't accept us, if there is a famine in the land—we call it an act of God.

In fact, as I was writing this book, a terrifying and powerful tornado hit Moore, Oklahoma. The news was everywhere, and the loss of homes and lives was tragic. One particular video that went viral was of a family that had been in a crawl space and then came out after the tornado. The husband holds the camera, and the darkness is washed out as he opens the storm hatch. He swings the camera left and right. What used to be a neighborhood is now a flattened scrap heap. For thirty seconds or so, he just walks around, surveying the devastation, staggered into silence by the scene. Finally he says, "The Lord giveth, and the Lord taketh away."

He was quoting Job (see Job 1:21). Remember him? Job experienced that level of devastation. But I couldn't help but notice the comment section underneath the video. There was a furious argument going on about whether or not this was God's fault. Some posted defending statements on God's behalf, citing verses about God's love and mercy. Others declared with great assurance that this was not God's fault but the Devil's. Others blamed it on Mother Nature, saying we live in a harsh world. When we don't know how to make sense of something or who to blame for it, God can become an easy target.

Honest About Responsibility

The Prodigal Son finally got honest about his reality and came out of denial. He agreed, "Here I am starving to death!" Then he took the next step. Instead of blaming everybody else, instead of projecting, he was honest about his responsibility.

"I have sinned," he said.

He didn't blame his dad. He didn't blame his friends. He didn't blame God. The son was brutally honest and told himself the truth. He opened his eyes and took responsibility.

If I hadn't rebelled against my father, I would have been well taken care of.

If I hadn't wasted all my money getting wasted, I would have been able to buy food and survive this terrible famine.

If I hadn't thought I knew better than everybody else, including God, I would be living the good life back home.

Instead of blaming everybody else for circumstances beyond his control, the son blamed the only person who made the choices that landed him in the pigpen in the distant country during the famine. He took responsibility for what he could control.

There's something beautiful about his short sentence. Those few spoken words finally set the son on a path to freedom. And they'll do the same for us.

Try this. Say these four words:

I am a sinner.

Say them again.

I am a sinner.

This is the path to freedom.

Chapter 8

MINIMIZE—IT'S NOT THAT BIG A DEAL

I was sitting in a coffee shop with my MacBook open on the table in front of me working on my sermon for the upcoming weekend. I was just wrapping it up when an older gentleman from the church came over. He set his large coffee cup on the table, extended his hand, and introduced himself to me. As he began to talk, he accidently knocked over his coffee, which spilled right onto my computer keyboard.[1] I watched in horror as twenty ounces of fresh coffee soaked my computer. The screen almost immediately flashed and went dark.

I looked at the man, and it was clear he didn't realize what he had done. "Oh, sorry about that," he said, chuckling. He tottered off to grab a fistful of napkins and returned to dab the keyboard and sop up the coffee. Meanwhile, I was in shock. Everything was in slow motion. It became an out-of-body experience. *Is this really*

---

1. I'm assuming it was an accident, but it's possible he just didn't like my preaching.

happening? kept flashing through my mind. Still on napkin duty, the old man tried to lighten the mood. He pointed to the logo on my Mac and said, "Looks like someone already took a bite out of that apple anyway."

He had a good laugh at that one.

I grabbed my computer, shut it, and practically ran away. I didn't even know where I was going. I could feel the coffee coming out of my computer and giving my hands what must have been third-degree burns. But I couldn't even feel it. All I could think of was everything on my hard drive that hadn't been backed up—including my sermon for the weekend.

A few days later the man called my office to apologize. "I hope your computer dried out, and it didn't end up being a big deal," he said. Mad as I was about it, I didn't have the heart to tell him the truth. He still jokes with me about it every now and then, because to him it was just a small accident.

That's minimization—though in this case, unintentional.

Denial is refusing to acknowledge the reality of a situation.

Projection is acknowledging the reality of the situation but denying any responsibility.

Minimization is acknowledging the reality of the situation and even owning responsibility for it—but denying its seriousness.

No Big Deal

Instead of being brutally honest, we tell ourselves half-truths that we can feel better about. "It's not that bad" is the favorite saying of minimization.

Have you ever seen *Monty Python and the Holy Grail*? It's only one of the most classic movies of all time. If you've seen it, you're already quoting lines like, "I'm not dead yet," and "Your mother was a hamster and your father smelt of elderberries." But the best line comes when, on his quest, King Arthur encounters the Black Knight. The Black Knight refuses to join Arthur and refuses to let him cross the bridge he is guarding. So they sword fight. It doesn't take long for Arthur to cut off the Black Knight's arm.[2] But the knight won't give up. Arthur chops off his other arm. And it's then that we get the comedic poetry. "It's only a flesh wound," the Black Knight says.[3]

That's minimization.

The Prodigal Son kept both his arms. But it's not until things were really bad that he finally told himself the truth—"Here I am starving to death"—and took responsibility for getting himself there—"I have sinned." He had plenty of opportunities to be honest with himself earlier, but he never seemed to realize the seriousness of his situation. Now in his moment of brutal honesty, he practiced a speech to give to his father when he got back home. And in the speech he didn't try to say "no big deal." He told the truth about where his sin and rebellion had led. He said, "Father, I have sinned against heaven and against you. I am no longer worthy to be called your son; make me like one of your hired servants" (Luke 15:18–19).

---

2. The spurting blood is hilariously fake. And yes, the video is on YouTube.

3. Terry Gilliam and Terry Jones, *Monty Python and the Holy Grail* (Python [Monty] Pictures, 1975).

I'm not sure who first said it, but there's an old saying that goes likes this:

> *Sin will always take you farther than you want to go.*
> *Sin will always cost you more than you want to pay.*
> *Sin will always keep you longer than you want to stay.*

The Bible doesn't minimize the consequences of sin. It shows us over and over again just how seriously God takes sin.

When God wanted to warn the people in the Old Testament that destruction was coming, He usually sent a prophet. The prophet would confront the people with the truth of where things were heading. But the people would often minimize the message and brush aside the warning. "It's not really that bad," they would say. Instead of repenting and turning back to God, they would continue down the same path. But when the people were brutally honest and turned away from from their sin, God would respond with compassion and grace.

Remember Jonah? After Jonah's detour in the exact opposite direction and moment of awakening inside a giant fish, Jonah reached Nineveh and gave the people God's message. Here's the sermon he preached: "Forty more days and Nineveh will be overthrown" (Jon. 3:4).

That may be the shortest sermon in the history of the world. It's only eight words long! In the original Hebrew language, it's only six words.[4] Jonah showed up with an unpopular message, not one that was going to bring a lot of people back to church. You'd think maybe

---

4. I actually checked. Pastors do that sort of thing.

he would have tried to start off with a joke or put together some cool visual aids. But Jonah didn't minimize the message.

Sometimes it's hard for pastors to say things that will upset people—at least it is for me. It's tempting to lighten things up and avoid words like *sin, sinner, hell,* and *punishment.* But maybe one of the reasons people minimize sin is because preachers don't seem to take it seriously either. Jonah wasn't worried about offending anybody in Nineveh. He went straight to the point: "You've got a little more than a month; then it's buh-bye, Nineveh."

So—how did the people of Nineveh respond? How would we?

Maximizing Minimization

We're good at minimizing. Instead of being honest, we downplay our responsibility; we brush off any thought of the consequences of our decisions. We don't use the word *minimization* every day, but we do minimize a lot. You'll probably recognize some of the following phrases—yep, they're all minimization in action.

I'm Just Having Fun

This is a popular saying in the Distant Country. The Prodigal Son spent all his money on wild living, but, hey, he was just having a good time. And we rationalize, "As long as I'm having fun and not hurting anyone, then it's all good."

There's a book called *Over the Edge: Death in Grand Canyon.* It's not what you'd call an uplifting read. Almost seven hundred people have died at the Grand Canyon since the 1870s, and this book describes each death. It doesn't surprise me that so many people have died there. What's surprising is *how* they died. A lot of people fell to their deaths because they were joking around.

In 1992 a thirty-eight-year-old father was joking around with his teenage daughter and pretended to lose his balance and fall. One second he was pranking his daughter, and suddenly the fake fall became very real. Tragically he stumbled a bit too far and fell four hundred feet to his death.

Then there was the eighteen-year-old young lady who was hiking around the North Rim with friends in 2012. She thought it would be fun to have her picture taken next to the Stay Away sign at the edge. You know— just to get an ironic Facebook picture to show she was a true adventurer. So she clambered out to the sign. Several rocks gave way, and she fell 1,500 feet.

It doesn't matter how many warning signs there are. Visitors wanting to have a little fun get too close to the edge.

As a pastor I see all kinds of people blow off warnings by minimizing consequences. They say, "I'm just having a little fun." But they don't realize that their actions are heading for the edge one fun step at a time. And the rocks will eventually give way. They always do.

The Prodigal Son was having a blast in the distant country, but he was closer to the edge than he realized.

A college student is shocked beyond tears as he listens to the judge's sentence: life in prison. Life—his whole life, his future, his career, his dreams—locked up, gone. A family is dead because he got behind the wheel and drove drunk. He can't believe this is happening to him. He shakes his head and says, "It was just some harmless partying."

The journey to the pigpen almost always starts by minimizing our sin.

Things Will Get Better

The son must have told himself this multiple times. When he was running low on money, when his food supply started to dwindle, when he couldn't find a decent job, maybe even his first day in the pigpen, he probably said, "It's not that bad; I'm sure things will get better." Another way I sometimes hear it is, "I'm sure things can't get any worse than this." I wonder if that's what Pharaoh told himself after each of the first nine plagues. We use this excuse as we spiral farther and farther down. We minimize instead of being brutally honest. We keep saying, "Things will get better," but the truth is that things have never been worse.

I have a friend who has struggled with a gambling addiction for a long time. It began as just a fun distraction. He would bet twenty bucks on a game now and then. Then one weekend he went with some buddies to Vegas and started playing the slot machines. He was down a few hundred dollars but kept telling himself, "Things will get better." By 4:00 a.m. he had lost more than $7,000 and drained his checking account. When he came home, he couldn't bring himself to tell his wife what happened. Besides, he was sure his luck would change, because things couldn't get much worse, right? He started spending more and more time at the horse races, which are popular here in Kentucky.

Fast-forward three years. He has maxed out thirteen credit cards. His gambling debts are in the millions. He has been fired for suspected embezzlement. His wife has moved out. His house is in foreclosure. But do you know what he said to me last time we talked? He said, "My luck is going to change; I can feel it." In other words, "Things will get better."

I can't help but wonder, *What's it gonna take?*

What's it gonna take for you to realize how bad things have gotten?

What's it gonna take to move away from the edge?

What's it gonna take for you to get some help for your addiction?

What's it gonna take for you to seek God's help?

Seriously, how far does this have to go?

It's Not That Big a Deal

This is probably what the Prodigal Son would have said if someone had tried to warn him about where his decisions were leading: "It's not that big of a deal." I hear this one a lot when confronting people about the choices they are making and where their path is leading.

Have you ever seen the TV show *Hoarders?* The show features people who are in danger of losing their homes, or even their kids, because so much junk has piled up in the house that it's not safe to live in anymore. The footage can be shocking. The camera crew opens the front door, and they can barely get inside the house. A small path winds through rooms packed wall-to-wall with newspapers, dirty clothes, composting food, unopened boxes, unidentifiable collectibles, and unrecognizable rotting trash.

I should mention I'm not the neatest or most organized person. So whenever I watch, I try to make sure my wife is paying attention, because this messiness makes me look really good.

But here's what I've noticed about *Hoarders*: there's always a point in the show when the host asks the hoarders about the state of their home. And almost always, they give one of two responses.

Sometimes they say, "I'm not sure how it got to be like this." But the even more common reply is, "I really don't think it's that bad."

They can't get into their bedroom. The bathroom can't be used. No one can see the bed or the table or the countertops or the floor, because everything is buried under piles and piles of stuff. But the hoarder says, "It's not that big a deal."

It sounds crazy, but we do it too. We don't realize how bad things are. That happens when you spend too much time in the Distant Country. You start to compare yourself to the people around you and say, "If everyone is living this way, then what's the big deal?" Before long, your perspective becomes warped. After enough time, the sin and rebellion don't seem like a big deal, because everyone is doing it. And when everyone around you is doing it, it's harder to be brutally honest about your own condition.

About ten years ago my family moved into a neighborhood where no one took great care of their lawns. We mowed when we got around to it. Nobody fertilized or specially treated their grass. We all seemed to have an unspoken agreement that dandelions were actually beautiful flowers—the more you had, the prettier your yard looked. And we were all quite content and happy living this way. Then one day a new neighbor moved in next door to me. We'll call him Jonah. And he began to take meticulous care of the grass. Have you ever had neighbors like that? They use dark magic to make their lawn have some checkered pattern like their lawn is a baseball diamond. That can't be from God. If God wanted grass to be checkered, He would have made it that way.

So you might think having a neighbor with a beautiful lawn would be great, but you know what? It was annoying. His yard revealed the truth about the rest of our yards. His commitment to excellence highlighted our commitment to mediocrity. And it just took the one neighbor coming in and holding up a different standard for the rest of us to be more honest about what a mess things had become.

God's Word should get our attention and help us see some things that are a bigger deal than we've realized.

180

Jonah was that one guy in Nineveh. When the people were confronted with Jonah's blunt truth, how they did they respond?

They didn't minimize the situation. They didn't say, "Oh, Jonah's exaggerating to get our attention. We're sure it won't be that bad."

They didn't say, "Forty days? That's plenty of time. We're sure things will get better."

They didn't say, "That sounds bad, but all that destruction and stuff—that's for other people. It doesn't apply to us."

Instead the people believed Jonah. And three words in the Bible changed everything for Nineveh: "The Ninevites believed …" (Jon. 3:5).

Jonah's message may have been hard to hear, but the people embraced the brutal honesty. In fact, everybody declared a fast and put on sackcloth.

Ever heard of sackcloth? You won't find it at Hollister. It's about as comfortable as it sounds. Sackcloth was a rough, scratchy covering made of goat hair—maybe like those coarse coffee sacks you sometimes see hanging in coffee shops. People in the Bible wore sackcloth in public as a sign of grieving and repentance. It sounds pretty crazy to us, but in Nineveh, even the rich and famous and powerful people did it after they heard Jonah's message. Try picturing Beyoncé or Justin Bieber doing this. Think about the president of the United States sitting on the White House lawn in this stuff.

Nineveh was part of a world power, and the greatest to the least of its people made this gesture of humility—even the king. And the king didn't stop there. He made a decree that not only did the people have to fast and wear sacks, but the animals did too. Can you imagine trying to put sackcloth on a cat? That's hard-core repentance.

The king also said, "Let everyone call urgently on God. Let them give up their evil ways and their violence. Who knows? God may yet relent and with compassion turn from his fierce anger so that we will not perish" (Jon. 3:8–9).

The people of Nineveh did not minimize God's message. They were brutally honest with themselves. They recognized that their sin was a big deal, and they responded to that truth by confessing and turning away from it.

And when God saw their changes, He forgave them.

Counting the Cost

The Prodigal Son reacted a lot like the Ninevites. Instead of telling himself, "It's no big deal," or "I'm sure things will get better," the Prodigal Son told himself the truth about himself. He didn't minimize his rebellion or the consequences he deserved. He finally saw that he'd made a string of bad decisions that had sent him over the edge. So he was done pretending. He was ready to count the cost of his choices. He planned to tell his father, "I'm no longer worthy to be called your son."

He recognized the relational damage he'd done. The Prodigal Son hadn't hurt only himself. He had wounded his father's pride and scarred their relationship in a way that should have been nearly irreparable. Now the son recognized the full weight of the emotional damage he had caused. He'd walked out on his father, his brother, his family, and his community. The relational bridges he'd once had were in ashes because of his choices.

And let's look for a minute at the practical cost of the son's choices. Forget the relationships for a minute. From a purely financial perspective, the son had totally altered his quality of living. He'd gone from rich party boy to starving pig boy—from riches to rags. And he knew he was probably stuck there for life. At best, he'd be able to scratch out a living as a hired hand if—and it was a big if—his father would even hire him back. He wasn't living in America, the land of opportunity. He was living in an ancient culture where wealth, status, and possibility came from one's family. When he burned through his inheritance, he burned through his future. Now it was gone. And so was hope of the provision and prosperity he would have had if he'd waited patiently. When the Prodigal Son totaled his bill for his stay in the distant country, he saw it had cost him everything.

Want to know what losing everything looks like today? I had a friend who was a pastor at a large church. He made some unfortunate mistakes, and they were displayed for the public. His choices cost him his job, his wife, and his family. The divorce was expensive enough, but as the dust settled from his disastrous fall, he took time to literally count the cost. He added up every economic asset and material possession he had lost, including the salary he would have earned from the job where he had planned to stay for a long time. It was well over half a million dollars. Not even counting the moral and relational consequences, my buddy realized that even in the most practical sense, his decisions had cost him everything.

That's brutal honesty, and AHA doesn't happen without it.

So what about you? Add up the bill. What's the cost of the choices you are making?

I don't know the exact consequences you're facing right now. I don't know exactly how you're minimizing them. And I don't know what warnings you're walking past on your way to the edge of the canyon.

But I do know there's a bill we should all have to pay. The Bible says, "The wages of sin is death" (Rom. 6:23). That's the bill for our sin. Our choice to sin has created a barrier between God and taken a toll on our relationship with Him that we can't fix, repair, or pay off on our own.

Let's not minimize the situation. Let's look at it with brutal honesty. We've offended the holy, righteous God who reigns in justice. We've broken His laws. Like the son, we've robbed honor from our Father. We've demanded our own way. We've blown off His provision and run away from His house. We have chosen wild living with strangers over a relationship with Him. Like the Prodigal Son, we've told God that it'd be better off if He were dead. We've pretended He doesn't exist and lived like it. We've chosen a path that leads to starvation, and that's what we deserve. We deserve death for what we've done.

But God gives us a chance. He offers us a brand-new inheritance. It's an inheritance that has been reclaimed and cashed in by His Son, Jesus Christ. Jesus came to earth and died for our sins to pay the bill. It was a big one when it was all totaled—it cost Jesus His life. But He was willing to pay it. He was raised to life after being crucified, and now He calls us to come home. He has a place waiting for us. The cost of our sin is more than we can ever repay, but God's grace through Jesus is more than enough to cover it.

PART 3
IMMEDIATE ACTION

So he got up …

Chapter 9

TIME TO GET UP

For our senior class trip, my high school class went to Dallas, Texas.[1] While we were there, I saw someone bungee jump for the first time. It was a relatively new phenomenon back then, and we all gathered around to watch. This wasn't just any bungee jump. It was one of the tallest in the country. The platform was several hundred feet off the ground. We watched as a guy got ready to make the leap with nothing but a cord strapped to his ankles. He dove off headfirst, and it was clear to me that my classmates were impressed.

It was in this moment that I experienced a phenomenon known as *word vomit*. It's when a thought spews from your mouth before you can stop it. Here's what came out: "I'd do that, but I'm not going to spend forty bucks on it."

I was trying to sound cool enough to go bungee jumping—but too cool to actually spend the money. After my declaration, there was

---

1. 52,321 more candy bars, and it would have been Los Angeles. So close.

a little commotion behind me. One of the girls in my class pulled out a twenty-dollar bill and said, "Would this help?"

At this point, my back was kind of against the wall. A girl had called my bluff—in front of everyone. Sure, I could've said, "Well, I'm not going to spend twenty bucks on it, either," but that wouldn't have gone over so well. So without stopping to consider the fact that I don't do well with heights, I took the twenty and stepped in line.

Here's the play-by-play.

As the crane was lowered, I watched and told myself, "It's not that high." But once the platform was at ground level and I stepped on board, I was inwardly racked with nervousness. I smiled at my classmates, trying to put out a vibe of uncaring amusement, my best Luke Perry[2] imitation. But I was freaking out inside.

The guy who was strapping the cord around my ankles did not inspire confidence. I'm pretty sure he was still wearing his 7-Eleven shirt from his other job. The platform was raised higher and higher, until finally the crane lurched to a halt. I stepped to the edge, the tips of my sneakers sticking out over the platform. I could faintly hear my friends cheering me on, and I instinctively made a horrible choice: I looked down. Suddenly, the full truth of my circumstances smacked me in the face. My friends, once life-size and within reach, were now mere specks on the distant, unforgiving surface of the earth, far, far away. And I was about to plummet toward them with nothing strapped to my body but a glorified rubber band, which

---

2. Don't question my choice of Luke Perry here. It was 1994. He was like the Keegan Allen or Ed Westwick of the day.

was harnessed to me by a man who, for all I knew, had been slinging Slurpees a few hours ago.

I had a white-knuckled death grip on the pole attached to the platform. I was overcome with paralyzing fear. "I can't do it. I just can't do it!" I screamed at—I mean, I smoothly and coolly suggested to—the crane operator. Then a thought struck me. "Would you just give me a shove?" I asked.

Apparently I wasn't the first kid who'd been too scared to jump but who was still too embarrassed to go down. "Well, we're not legally allowed to push someone off," the bungee worker said.

Frustrated with this reply—*Thanks for being such a rule follower, Mr. 7-Eleven*—I asked, "Do you have any other ideas for me here?"

"Well, sometimes it works if you just close your eyes and fall," he said, adding, "Anybody can do that."

Well, fine, I thought, mustering some courage—any courage that might be hidden somewhere inside the paralyzed reaches of my soul. *That sounds all right. I can do that. I can fall.*

So I stepped to the edge, closed my eyes, and I'm proud to say that—well, I didn't so much bungee jump, but I did bungee *fall* that day.

Unstuck

It's one thing to say what you're going to do, and it's another thing to do it. Action is where a lot of us get stuck. We know what needs to be done. We have stepped out onto the platform. But we just.can't.move. It's one thing to have the awakening. It's one thing even to be honest about what you need to do. It's another thing to take the leap.

Maybe this is a helpful picture: Think of AHA as a door that swings on three hinges. The first hinge is a sudden awakening. The second hinge is brutal honesty. The third and final hinge is immediate action.

In Jesus's parable of the prodigal son, there's a simple phrase that changes the story: "So he got up …" (Luke 15:20).

The Prodigal Son took immediate action. He saw that it was time to get up. It was time to do something. And unless our stories read, "So he got up" or "So she got up," then nothing really changes. But this is where AHA stalls out for so many of us. We have an awakening moment. We even find the strength to be brutally honest. But we never get around to actually doing anything different. We spend much of our lives stuck between honesty and action.

So He Got Up … From the Couch

Have you ever made a goal, a New Year's resolution, or a wish to get in better shape? Then you know what we're talking about. Here's how it goes.

First There Is a Sudden Awakening …
Something happens to awaken us from our current condition.

You try to put on those jeans but can't get them buttoned.

You get up for a rare break from your video game console and realize there's a permanent imprint of your, uh, seat on the couch.

You decide to get some exercise and start breathing hard before you even get outside.

For me the moment came when I was at Starbucks getting my grande vanilla Frappuccino—with no whip, I might add. As I was paying, a coin fell out of my pocket and onto the ground. Instead of immediately bending over to pick it up, I looked down to see how much the coin was worth. Because if it were a penny, bending over to pick it up wouldn't be worth it; that'd be too much work. If it were a quarter … well, that would be worth the intense physical exertion required to bend over. When I saw that it was a nickel, I stood there for ten seconds debating whether it was worth it. Okay, so I'm old; I admit it. But that was an awakening for me.

Next Comes the Brutal Honesty …

You tell yourself the hard truth about yourself.

You step on the scale.

You talk to your mom about genuine health and body images, not unreal expectations like airbrushed magazine models.

And you honestly assess your diet and eating habits and begin to write down how many calories you consume throughout the day.

You add up everything and tell yourself the truth.

Now It's Time for Immediate Action …

Now comes the real test.

You come home from school. You're tired. The Xbox is calling, as are the frozen mozzarella sticks and Southwestern egg rolls. But you know you've got a date with your running shoes—or with Jillian Michaels, Bob Harper, Tony Horton, or whoever your celebrity trainer of choice is.[3] So what are you going to do? Will you take action? Or will you head back to that couch?

Change or Die

Sadly, knowing that A + B = C doesn't always equal C for us. We can know we *need* to change, but that doesn't always mean we're *gonna* change. I read an article that began with this paragraph:

> Change or Die. What if you were given that choice? … What if a well-informed, trusted authority figure said you had to make difficult and enduring changes in the way you think and act? If you didn't, your time would end soon—a lot sooner than it had to. Could you change when change really mattered? When it mattered most?[4]

According to the article, the odds are nine to one against your changing—even in the face of certain death. The author based that statistic on a well-known study by the dean of the medical school at Johns Hopkins University, Dr. Edward Miller.

Dr. Miller studied patients whose heart disease was so bad that they had to undergo bypass surgery. That's the surgery where they cut you

---

3. You know—they're the trainers from *The Biggest Loser* and P90X. I can't prove it, but I'm certain there is a direct correlation between how annoying a person is and how effective they are as a trainer.

4. Alan Deutschman, "Change or Die," *Fast Company*, May 1, 2005, http://www .fastcompany.com/52717/change-or-die.

open and split your rib cage apart to work on your heart. It's traumatic to your body and your wallet. It can cost more than $100,000 if complications arise. About 600,000 Americans have bypasses every year. And another 1.3 million people have angioplasties. At least for an angioplasty, they don't have to split open your chest. We're used to hearing about all kinds of crazy medical procedures, but they're really amazing when you think about it. Heart bypasses and angioplasties give patients a second chance. With some lifestyle changes, these patients can now prolong their lives—if they're willing to act on the opportunity.

But Dr. Miller says those people rarely make any changes. His research checked in with patients two years after they had bypass surgery. And 90 percent of them did *not* change their lifestyles. These are people who almost died. They got a second chance.

"Even though they know they have a very bad disease and they know they should change their lifestyle, for whatever reason, they can't," Dr. Miller said in the article.

In our lives, awakening calls attention to our heart disease—we realize something is wrong. And then we have to allow brutal honesty to do its work in our hearts, essentially bypassing the lies we've believed or told ourselves. Then we, like the heart patients, have an opportunity to act.

To put it another way: awakening happens to us. Honesty happens in us. But nothing really changes unless action comes from us.

Confusing Feelings for Action

Here's something I've learned: we sometimes get stuck between honesty and action because we confuse our feelings with actually doing something. We trick ourselves. We believe that because we *feel* differently about something, we are actually doing something—even though we haven't actually done anything yet. So we spend our lives with good intentions and strong feelings, but we never actually get around to leaving the pigpen.

Recognizing and feeling bad about our mistakes—conviction—is always an invitation to action. But when the conviction in our heart doesn't lead to a change in our lives, then we suffer from some consistent side effects. See if you experience any of these symptoms—and take them as a warning sign that you need some action.

Fatigue and Frustration

A sudden awakening is an invitation to align your life with what's happening in your heart. But when you don't take action, your life is violating your heart. From my own personal experience and from listening to other people's stories, I can tell you that when your actions violate your convictions, there is a general underlying sense of fatigue and frustration.

It's exhausting to try to live in a way that violates your heart. It leaves you constantly drained. Even the American Heart Association gets it. Seriously. The American Heart Association says to relieve stress, "Examine your values and live by them. The more your actions reflect your beliefs the better you will feel."[5]

So imagine you wake up one day and check the news. A marathon is happening in town. *Why not? I'll run it,* you decide. But you

---

5. "How to Manage Your Stress," *USA Today*, March 7, 2001, usatoday30 .usatoday.com/news/health/2001-03-07-stress-tips.htm.

haven't been training for this race. You haven't even run around the block in a few years. What's going to happen? You're not going to make it to the finish line of the marathon. And you're going to be in a lot of pain. Your body is going to be violating your heart for however many miles you manage to struggle through.

When our actions violate our hearts, we inevitably end up fatigued and frustrated. Those feelings won't go away until you align your actions with the awakening of your heart.

Tension in Relationships

When you know what you need to do, but you haven't done it yet, it's only a matter of time until your frustration spills out onto others. If your life isn't aligned with your convictions, you'll be a hard person to live with.

This often shows up as a critical spirit. Know somebody who is always criticizing someone or something? He's revealing that there are some things about himself that need to be addressed, and he knows it.

Sometimes this frustration shows up in a relationship when a person is overly defensive. You can get pretty sensitive and defensive when you feel guilty about not taking an action you know you should take. And this kind of defensiveness will come out in other areas. You might lose your temper because of something totally unrelated to the action you need to take. You just give people a "What's that supposed to mean?" attitude, no matter what.

Undirected Anger

An awakening without action always leads to guilt. You feel guilty that you aren't living your life in a way that's consistent with your beliefs and values. Here's what's important to understand about guilt: it almost always comes out as anger.

Sometimes I talk to people who struggle with a general sense of anger. They're not really angry toward a certain person or about a specific situation. They're just angry in general. They try to dismiss it. They say, "That's just the way I am. I'm just wired that way."

If that describes you, let me ask you a question. Don't get mad at me, but is it possible that the reason you can't identify whom you're angry at is because you're actually angry with yourself? Maybe you feel guilty because you've been awakened to something, but you haven't done anything about it.

Where We Get Stuck

Immediate action may be where most of us get stuck, but it's important to recognize that without action, the story never changes. Look at this connection between two of the verses in Jesus's story in Luke 15:

> He came to his senses ... (v. 17)
> So he got up ... (v. 20)

Without verse 20, verse 17 doesn't really matter.

"So he got up" sounds so simple that it's easy to miss. But if the Prodigal Son hadn't gotten up, then he would have just stayed in the pigpen, aware that he was living in brokenness.

Michael Novak is a Catholic philosopher who made the point that until there is action, our beliefs and convictions aren't genuine. He describes three different levels of belief.

There are public beliefs. Those are the beliefs we try to get other people to think we believe. So we talk about helping the poor or protecting unborn lives, but we just want people to think those are our values—or we think we're supposed to have those beliefs.

There are also private beliefs. Novak explains that these are what we sincerely believe. Well, at least we sincerely believe that we believe them. But when these beliefs are tested, we discover we don't really believe.

Last there are core beliefs. These are ultimately the only true beliefs we hold, because they're backed up by reality. These aren't just something we say. They're more than just something we feel. These are how we live. Our core convictions are determined by the actions we take.

Don't tell me what your beliefs and values are; get up and show me.

Don't tell me that you care about the poor—get up, log onto Compassion International's website, and sponsor a child.

Your convictions aren't really worth anything until there is action.

If the Prodigal Son had come to his senses but had never gotten up, his story wouldn't have changed. If you're stuck between verses 17 and 20, then it's time to get up.

It's not easy to get up. I get that. But it's simple. Sometimes we have this complicated mess, and we want to address the complicated mess with a complicated plan, but the truth is really as simple as, "So he got up."

The journey home for the Prodigal Son would have been difficult. It would not have been easy to travel from this distant country on an empty stomach. But the son got up and went.

A girl comes to church who hasn't been close to God for a long time. Life in the Distant Country has taken its toll. She is full of regret. The past is full of pain, and honestly, she's having a hard time seeing much hope for the future. She's been drinking a lot. And she can't even remember some of the stuff she's done when she was drunk. She's finally being honest with herself about what her life has become. What she needs to do next won't be easy, but it isn't complicated. My prayer is that the next part of her story would read, "So she got up."

A guy deletes the history on his computer. He turns it off and promises himself, "Never again." He's been living with guilt and regret over his sin for years. He's had a few awakening moments, and he's been honest with how out of control his lust has become. But he has never really done anything to change it. When he catches me after a church service, he leans in close and says quietly, "I've never told this to anyone before, but I really do need help." Now that he's confessed it, I'm hoping the next part of his story reads, "So he got up."

My question for you is: When are you going to get up?

When are you going to get up and say to a friend, "I've been able to keep it a secret, but I have a problem and I need help"?

When are you going to get up and end the relationship you know God wants you to end?

When are you going to get up and be generous the way that you know God has called you to be generous?

When are you going to get up and ask for forgiveness from the parents you've wounded so many times?

When are you going to get up and join a small group or Bible study for the first time in your life?

When are you going to get up and talk to one of your friends about faith?

When are you going to get up and do something real about all the social justice causes you post about online?

When is verse 20 going to be a part of your story?

It's time to get up.

Chapter 10

PASSIVITY—I'M SURE EVERYTHING WILL WORK ITSELF OUT

Fire season is a problem in Southern California. You've probably seen news and videos. When strong winds mix with the dry conditions, firestorms can get dangerous quickly. My family lived in Los Angeles, and we've had ash fall in our backyard. My kids would ask, "Is that snow?"

A few months after we moved away, a severe firestorm spread to the hills right behind our old house. We could see our old neighborhood on the news.

There was an article in *USA Today* titled "Hesitation Is a Fatal Mistake as California Firestorm Closes In."[1] It talked about people who were warned of this fire in advance but wouldn't leave their homes. They even watched the news about how close the fires were getting but waited too long to leave. That firestorm claimed over two dozen lives. In the article Sergeant Conrad Grayson of the San Diego County Sheriff's Department said, "We're begging people to leave, and they don't take us seriously. They want to pack some clothes, or fight it in the backyard with a garden hose."

A resident named Jon Smalldridge told of frantically warning his neighbors as flames swept into the neighborhood. Some people casually brushed him off. Some people wanted to get their TVs and computers first. "They looked like they were packing for a trip," Smalldridge said. "The ones who listened to me and left the area, lived. The ones who didn't, died."

Seriously? Would you die for your TV? What is it that keeps us from acting with a greater sense of urgency? Instead of being aggressive, it seems easier or more natural for us to respond passively. Even when fire is threatening and our lives are at risk, we tend to have an "I'm sure everything will work itself out" attitude.

By this point in Jesus's story, the Prodigal Son was over that. He didn't just hope that his luck would change. He didn't wait for the famine to end and the economy to turn around. He came up with a plan of action. He said to himself, "I will set out, and go back to

---

1. Scott Bowles, "Hesitation Is a Fatal Mistake as California Firestorm Closes In," *USA Today*, October 30, 2003, usatoday30.usatoday.com/news/nation/2003 -10-30-fires-usat_x.htm.

my father, and say to him …" (Luke 15:18). He did the opposite of saying, "I'll just sit down, stay here, and hope for the best."

And … Action

Here's an interesting irony about our society: we love action, but we'd rather watch it than live it. We kick back on the couch and order pizza—while we watch gourmet-cooking shows. We watch the Home Improvement Network for hours—then get ourselves a drink from a leaky faucet. We lie there watching contestants on *The Biggest Loser* push themselves to complete exhaustion—then watch whatever's on next because we don't want to get out of our La-Z-Boy to get the remote, which is across the room.

Okay, guys, honest moment. We tend to be especially good at being passive. But we also love action movies. Try this: How many movies have you seen in the last six months? How many of them were action movies? Uh-huh.

So, guys, I want to test your manliness. Okay, that sounds a little awkward, but you know what I mean. I'll give you a quote, and you name the action movie. Some of these are classics, but they're among the greatest action flicks ever.

> "Fight and you may die. Run and you'll live—at least a while. And dying in your beds many years from now, would you be willing to trade all the days—from this day to that—for one chance, just one chance, to come back here and tell our enemies that they may take our lives, but they'll never take

our freedom!"[2] (HINT: Go back and read this with a Scottish accent.)

"I don't know who you are. I don't know what you want. If you are looking for ransom, I can tell you I don't have money. But what I do have are a very particular set of skills; skills I have acquired over a very long career. Skills that make me a nightmare for people like you."[3]

"The worst thing that happened to you, that can happen to any fighter: you got civilized."[4]

"You're not just anyone. One day, you're going to have to make a choice. You have to decide what kind of man you want to grow up to be. Whoever that man is—good character or bad—is going to change the world."[5]

"What we do in life echoes in eternity."[6] (To feel more like a man, start off each day by looking in

---

2. *Braveheart*
3. *Taken*
4. *Rocky III*
5. *Man of Steel*
6. *Gladiator*

the mirror and yelling this. Bonus points if you do
so with an Australian accent.)

We love to *watch* action. Don't tell my wife, but I secretly watch
the UFC fights on Sunday nights after a long weekend of preaching.
When men witness that kind of action, something comes alive in
us. We're inspired by the fighter who refuses to quit, by the battled
soldier who rushes the enemy, by the athlete who rallies the team
against all odds.

But when the movie ends, what do we do? Instead of fighting for
a girl's honor, we just stand there and let a mean kid or our culture
walk all over her. Instead of being passionate about our relationship
with God, we get passionate about a new video game. Instead of
fighting against temptation, we tap out and say it's too much. Instead
of taking a stand, we lie on the couch flipping through four thousand
DISH channels.

Inaction in Our Blood

I'm not trying to beat you up over this. It's partly wired into you,
guys. You could even say it's the first sin we inherited from Adam.
The Bible says that back during the whole Eve and the serpent thing,
Adam was right there, just watching and listening while a snake
talked his wife into doing exactly what God had told them not to do.
Check it out in Genesis 3:6. Adam said nothing. He did nothing. He
just stood there.

And Adam wasn't the only Bible guy guilty of passivity. Maybe
you've heard of Eli. He was a priest and judge of Israel. In other

words, he was the top leader for a while. But he also had two sons, Hophni and Phinehas. They were priests, too, since they were his sons. But—and this is a problem for a priest—the Bible says they were wicked and didn't care anything about God (1 Sam. 2:12). They totally abused their position. They didn't just ignore God; they stole from the offering. They swiped the sacrifices, too—the animals people brought to God. That's kind of like walking into the Oval Office and robbing the president in broad daylight with no mask on—and getting away with it. Oh, and they slept with the women who worked at the tabernacle. They couldn't care less about God or anything He said.

So you might think their dad, Eli, the top leader and priest, didn't know what was going on; otherwise he'd put a stop to it, right? But Eli knew exactly what was happening. He got messages and complaints from others. Those reports were an awakening moment for him. People spoke the truth to him about what was happening; people brought him brutal honesty.

It was time for Eli to take some action. Dad was gonna lay down the law, take away the sons' power, and make things right. Right? He talked to them. And … uh … that's about it. That's all the action he took. He gave them what my fellow Kentuckians would call "a good talkin' to." He acted like what Dr. Phil calls a "threatening parent." A parent who's always saying, "Well, next time …" or "If you do that again …" or "This time I mean it …"

They probably laughed about it after Eli left. "Ooooh, Dad's getting scary! Now, where'd those women go? Pass me another leg o' lamb." They kept right on doing what they'd been doing.

And Eli did nothing.

Mixed-Up Priorities

So what was Eli's deal? How come the leader of the nation was so passive? The Bible gives us a clue. It's easy to miss, but it's important in understanding why we also choose passivity over action. God asked Eli, "Why do you honor your sons more than me?" (1 Sam. 2:29). When God warned Eli about his sons, Eli did nothing. He chose his sons over God.

Don't miss this: our passive approach to the action God has called us to shows that we care about something else more than we care about Him.

God convicts you about a dating relationship—but you don't do anything. Why? Because you care about your boyfriend or girlfriend more than you care about God.

He convicts you about lust—but you don't take any action, because you value your desires more than you value God.

God convicts you about being generous—but you don't give anything, because you honor your money and time more than you honor God.

He convicts you to stand up and be a leader—but you sit back while people mock God and His followers, because you're more concerned about what people think about you than what God thinks about you.

Passivity reveals that we are choosing something or someone over God.

Eli got another chance to shake off passivity and take action to make things right. But he still didn't take it. God sent him a messenger with a warning that basically said, "Last chance, Eli. If you're not going to make things right, I am. Your sons are going to pay up, and I'm going to get everyone's attention."

So you'd think the story would change here—Eli would turn from his wrongs and get up. Nope. Eli said, "He is the LORD; let him do what is good in his eyes" (1 Sam. 3:18).

That may sound superspiritual, like Eli was being submissive to God's will. But Eli was just being passive. He'd just found out that his family and any future generations in his family were going to experience long-term consequences. He was a priest. He studied God's Word. He knew there were many times when God showed mercy to people who turned from wrong and sought His forgiveness.

Eli should have been willing to come before God in brokenness and to stand and act on behalf of his family. Instead he sat back and said, "Whatever, God. I can't do anything about it."

Ice Cream in the Shade

Most of us have good intentions, but too many of us have ended up like Eli. But he's not the only passive one in the story. He seems to have passed it on to his sons. They were warned and threatened, but they never made any changes. While Eli's passivity may have come more from laziness or apathy, his sons' passivity seems to have come from arrogance.

These two guys grew up with a sense of entitlement. You might have heard it thrown around about your generation. Maybe you don't think such an assessment is fair, or maybe you know kids who make you say, "Uh, yep. There are definitely some spoiled people around these days."

Either way, entitlement is nothing new. Eli's sons knew from the day they were born that they'd be priests, an honored position in Israel. They didn't have to earn it. They were handed the good life. They grew up pampered and well taken care of, and they expected everything to be handed to them. That's entitlement, and it often leads to passivity. They didn't appreciate what they had. They thought they deserved it. And they did whatever they wanted and expected everything to work out fine.

This kind of entitled passivity says, "Who cares? I'll end up with the things I want whether I try or not."

I saw this on full display at Holiday World this past summer. It was a long, hot day, and the misery of waiting in line usually wasn't worth the fun of the ride.

But I was waiting in line with my kids for a roller coaster, and there was this middle-aged woman in front of me who was in line by herself. That seemed a bit strange, but good for her. Maybe she was trying to stay young. Then I saw her mouthing words and using hand motions to communicate with someone far away. I realized she was talking to a teenage boy who was eating Dippin' Dots under the shade of a tree.

It took me a few seconds to process what was going on. Apparently Mom was waiting in line alone while her teenage son ate ice cream in the shade. How was this happening? And how had he trained her so well? I was simultaneously appalled and amazed by the whole thing.

We kept waiting in line, and sure enough, she motioned him to come over as we got ready to get on the roller coaster. Well, this wasn't going to happen on my watch. There was no way this twerp, who'd been eating ice cream in the shade, was going to cut in line. I understand grace and mercy, but I also believe in justice. I was getting ready to say something, but the woman realized I wasn't happy about the situation. We locked eyes, and she said, "No, no. He's not cutting in line. I'm just waiting in line *for him* because it's such a hot day, but I'm not actually going to ride."

This baffled me further. So she was waiting in line on a hot day in the middle of summer for a ride she wasn't going to ride while her pampered teen sat in the shade shoveling Dippin' Dots into his mouth before riding a roller coaster that would probably make him puke out the dots and dips? I thought, *This kid is going to be so disappointed when he finds out they don't serve ice cream in the pigpen.* Because that's where entitled passivity leads you.

Cheat Codes

The Prodigal Son wasn't much different from the roller-coaster kid or Eli's two boys. His entitled outlook led him to ask for his own inheritance well before he deserved it. He didn't want to work alongside his father and tend to their estate. He'd rather skip the hard work and just get his payout. This was a passive move of him trying to dodge having to earn a living, and it was a passivity that honored money and good times over his relationship with his father. That was a big part of what he was communicating: "Dad, I wish you were dead so I could just have my money."

Once he got his cash, the son headed to the distant country, spent his money willy-nilly,[7] and threw weeklong parties that started early and finished late. He was entitled in his entertainment, and he was passive about his budgeting. He never took action or showed any kind of initiative to invest his inheritance wisely. He treated his money with a passive indifference. To the son, the father was just a means to get some money, and the money was just a means to have a good time. This is what passivity does to us. In our attempt to avoid any real action, we look for the quickest work-around, unaware that we're not only cheating others but also trying to cheat life.

Read this carefully and see if you recognize it:

Up, up, down, down, left, right, left, right, B, A, start.

Can you identify this code? It comes from the Nintendo[8] game *Contra*, one of my favorite games growing up. I loved *Contra*, but I could never beat it. There was this one part of the game I just couldn't get past. Then one day my friend Brian Jennings came over to my house and blew my mind. When the game turned on, he entered this

---

7. One of my editors said, "Do you really want to use the phrase *willy-nilly*? That seems a little too Kentucky."

My response: Consider the etymology of *willy-nilly*. The early meaning of the word *nil* was considered the opposite of will. So *will* means to want something and *nil* is to avoid or purposely ignore. So by combining *willy* with *nilly*, a person is communicating that something doesn't matter one way or the other. The earliest version of *willy-nilly* dates back at least a millennium and was a phrase that Shakespeare was fond of. Ex. *The Taming of the Shrew*.

8. You can separate the generations by their gaming systems. I go back to Nintendo, the greatest of all consoles. In my opinion, it's not a real gaming system if you don't have to blow on the cartridge to make it work.

code—up, up, down, down, left, right, left, right, B, A, start—and he got thirty free lives. Through some coercion and torture methods, he gave me this cheat, too, and it changed the way I played. From then on, I didn't even have to try hard. I assumed everything would work out because I had the cheat code.

Passivity looks for the shortcut, for the cheat, for the way around. But immediate action moves directly.

Passivity looks for the path of least resistance—the wide path. Immediate action looks for the path of righteousness—the narrow one.

Passivity wants to cheat. Action wants to change.

Passivity says, "Everything will work itself out." Action says, "This is going to take some work."

Passivity says, "What's the least I can get away with?" Action says, "What needs to be done?"

The son was passive in every aspect of his journey from his father's house to the distant country. But we do have to give him a little credit. He did finally act. He rejected passivity, made a game plan, and followed through.

Action is that simple and that difficult. Let's be honest: it's not easy to get up and walk home when you've been picked up and carried your whole life.

Action Steps

So maybe you're reading this chapter and you agree with me. You see some passivity in your own life. You know you need to change. Maybe you've been entitled. Maybe you have not been a man or woman of action. But maybe you think, *I agree with you, but I just don't feel like doing anything about it.*

I know how you feel. And while it may sound a little cold or trite, the truth is we need to obey God even when we don't feel like it. When we obey God even without feeling motivated, eventually our feelings will catch up with our actions.

I remember learning this lesson in California. One thing that really stresses me out is traffic. And California has plenty of traffic. One day I was stuck, surrounded by cars not going anywhere. I was riding the bumper of the car in front of me. I was honking my horn, hoping that somebody miles up the road would hear it and decide to go a little faster. I kept switching lanes, trying to move ahead a few extra feet. I was completely stressed.

I knew this wasn't what God wanted for me. He wants me to be at peace. I didn't feel at peace, so I decided to act like it and see what would happen. So I thought, *What would I do if I were at peace?*

Well, for starters I would back off the guy in front of me. I would quit honking my horn, and I wouldn't switch lanes. Okay, I backed off. I thought a man at peace might listen to some worship music. So I put some music on. A man at peace would probably sing along, so I started to sing. A man at peace might smile, so I forced myself to smile. A man at peace might wave at somebody, so I waved. I thought a man at peace would probably let someone else in front of him. But it's hard to say for sure, so I didn't do that one.

I don't know when it happened, but at some point I began to feel at peace. You see, our attitudes and emotions can catch up with our actions. We are called to be obedient even when we don't feel like it. I'm not saying be fake, but I am saying take obedient steps of action even if you don't feel like it at first.

So what's the game plan for the changes you need to make? You've probably made the list before, whether on paper or in your mind. Identify the first step, just like the son did. For him it was, "I will set out and go back to my father ..." He knew what he needed to do, and he followed through. Find your first step and act on it now, whether you feel like it or not. You may find that along the road, with God's help, actions that feel artificial at first can become authentic.

There's a guy in the Bible named Nehemiah who's a good contrast to Eli and his sons and the Prodigal Son's early behavior. Nehemiah got action right. He led God's people in an effort to rebuild the walls of Jerusalem. It was a huge job, and it reached a point where the work seemed to be too much. Enemies were harassing the workers, and the opposition seemed overwhelming. But Nehemiah didn't say, "Whatever. I guess it's too big of a problem." He called the men of Israel to be men of action. He challenged them and said, "Did you think this was going to be easy? Did you think the wall was going to just build itself?" And then the real action-movie movement comes. He said to them, "Pick up a sword and fight."

Guys—and girls, too—when will you pick up swords and fight? Put down the remote control, pick up a sword, and fight for justice for the children who are slaves around the world making the clothes hanging in your closet. Put down the smartphone, pick up a sword, and fight for love in your family relationships and in the hallways of your school. Put down the PlayStation controller; put down the iPad; pick up a sword and fight for *something*. It may even be time to put down this book. You've heard enough. It's time to stop reading, watching, talking, and playing. It's time for action.

Chapter 11

PROCRASTINATION—I'LL GET TO IT LATER.

[INTRO NEEDED HERE]

That note has been at the top of this chapter for weeks now. Whenever I write a book, I always want to make sure the chapters open with interesting stories. The kind of anecdotes that reel you in and make a compelling point at the same time. You've noticed that, right? Okay, just checking. The last thing I'd want to do is start by just defining the word *procrastination* for you.[1] No, you deserve a homespun tale or an intriguing piece of trivia. But those stories don't always come easily, so sometimes I just make the above note so I can move on and come back to it later.

Unfortunately, the final draft of this manuscript has to go to the publisher tomorrow, and I still don't have an opener for this chapter.

---

1. Dictionary.com defines *procrastination* as "the act or habit of procrastinating, or putting off or delaying, especially something requiring immediate attention."

I just kept assuming I would get to it. But now here we are. You're reading this book, and I'm still short an intro. You're experiencing the consequences of my procrastination. My bad.

You see, that's the thing about telling ourselves, "I'll get to it later." We tell ourselves that enough times and soon the urgency is gone. Inevitably our procrastination affects others.

Now or Never

The Prodigal Son may have procrastinated early in his story. Procrastination and denial go well together. *I'll count my money later,* he might have thought. *I'll figure out a way to make some more later. I can worry about that stuff tomorrow.*

But once the son made his plan, there was no procrastinating. He put it in motion immediately. Jesus said, "So he got up" (Luke 15:20). The word *so* indicates a quick response. It shows a continuation of the son's process. He said, "Here's what I'm gonna do," and then he got up and did it. He didn't put it off a day. He didn't waste time until the weather was good for traveling. He took action immediately.

Too many times after we have an awakening and honest moment, we sit in the pigpen trying to come up with a plan or promising ourselves that we'll take action sometime soon. Procrastination is one of Satan's favorite tools to prevent AHA from happening in your life. He knows that if you put off taking action long enough, you'll go back to sleep.

And it's effective, because even though we are still sitting in the pigpen, we feel like we've done something. Procrastination lets us off the hook because we're not saying no; we're just saying, "Not right now." We're not turning off the alarm; we're just hitting the snooze button. All we want is ten more minutes. Ten more minutes won't hurt anything. So we close our eyes and go back to sleep, because we have every intention of getting up—just not right now.

Here are a few reasons why we procrastinate so much:

We Want to Put Off the Pain

Those workout commercials where everyone appears happy and relaxed are funny. You've seen them, haven't you? A sweatless woman walks on a treadmill. A man works the weight machine as easily as if he were turning pages in this book. They look so calm, as if working out requires no exertion and is just a fun way to kill time. We all know that's a lie, but it's hard not to get swept into the idea of effortless fitness and pain-free progress. We think, *Just ten minutes a day, and I'll have abs like hers,* or *In just a couple of months I'll smile fifteen pounds away.*

But when you go to the gym, what are people doing? They're grunting and groaning, straining with determination, and contorting their faces into comically embarrassing expressions. It's never as easy as they make it look in the commercials, right? If things were really that easy, we'd all head to the gym and start pumping iron. If it were that pain-free, we would act. And most of us don't want to act, because we don't want the pain. So we put it off.

We put off the workouts, because we don't want sore muscles.

We put off hard conversation, because we don't want awkward tension.

We put off getting help, because we don't want to feel vulnerable.

We put off asking for forgiveness, because we don't want to be embarrassed.

The Prodigal Son knew how hard it was going to be to make the trip back home. He knew how painful it would be to see the disappointment in his father's eyes. He knew how humbling it would be to feel judged and condemned by his older brother. He knew it would be painful. He knew it would be shaming. He knew it would be difficult. But waiting wasn't going to make it any easier. In fact, the longer he put off action, the more difficult it would become. *So he got up.*

We Want to Prolong the Pleasure

Be honest. Being in the Distant Country and spending all kinds of money on wild living sounds kind of fun. We sometimes like to talk and act like sin isn't fun, like it doesn't ever feel good or bring any happiness. But the truth is that it often does. It doesn't last, and it ultimately brings much greater pain. But for a while it's fun. People sleep around and get hammered or high because they experience some earthly pleasure. You'll hear them give reasons like, "It makes me feel good," or "It helps me blow off some steam," or "I love how it feels to be wanted by someone." Those are honest responses about why they turn to sex, drugs, gambling, alcohol, and other habits. And even if we know deep down that these kinds of choices are going to lead to the pigpen, we think we still have time to enjoy them. And until the famine comes, we put off any action. *I can live it up a while longer,* we think. *Nothing bad has happened yet.*

Unfortunately, this kind of procrastination often has the opposite effect. It makes things worse. What if the Prodigal Son were living in our culture? He would have run out of money, but then he probably would have maxed out as many credit cards as he could to keep the party going. How much more does that complicate his story? How much worse would it have been for the son to arrive home buried in debt? Picture him saying, "Father, I've sinned against heaven and against you. I have no money, and by the way some creditors are coming, and I owe twice what my inheritance was worth."

The longer we try to prolong the pleasure, the greater the pain will be.

I read an article about how professional athletes deal with retirement. Most of us will work forty years in order to retire for twenty. Pro athletes will work for ten or fifteen years if they are lucky and then retire for fifty. But many athletes live extravagant lifestyles, and it catches up with them once they retire. Instead of cutting back and making some changes, they try to prolong the pleasure. One of the players I read about got paid over $100 million to play, and now he's broke. He owes almost a million dollars to his personal jeweler. What's even crazier is that he has a deferred payment coming to him in another two decades for $30 million in sponsorships. He's broke right now, but in twenty years he'll have another $30 million. So he keeps borrowing now against a payment he won't receive for a long time. He keeps spending and racking up debt. He's prolonging the pleasure, but the later pain will be that much greater.

Procrastination is the kind of habit that almost always catches up with you in a bad way. If it's not debt, it could be further damage to your relationships. You might keep hanging with the wrong crowd, and the next party will end with a court appearance, not just a hangover. I don't mean to sound dramatic, but as a pastor, I see this way too often. I hear too many stories. I've gotten too many late-night phone calls. I've had to sit with too many crying parents and spouses. Situations go from bad to worse and from worse to tragic because someone tried to prolong the pleasure. The extra week of wild living is never worth the lifelong consequences.

We Want the Perfect Plan

The son's plan of action wasn't complicated. It was pretty simple. Get up, go home, talk to his father. He didn't plan a pit stop to get cleaned up. He didn't plan a way to earn a little money so he wasn't going home broke. He didn't complicate the plan with any unnecessary steps.

Keeping it simple can be hard for us. But when you try to tie up every possible loose end, you just end up frustrated and convinced you need to work harder at the solution instead of actually reaching the solution. Sometimes we need a simple—not perfect—plan of action to cut through the knots.

A church was recently going through a series on relationships, and they asked me to come preach on the topic of sexual intimacy. That's kind of a sensitive topic, right? Especially as a guest speaker. So I was talking to my wife, and I said, "You know, of all the topics, why'd they give me this one?" And my wife said, "Sometimes they've got to call in an expert."[2]

So I went to preach on sexual intimacy. Afterward a college student who was about twenty-one came up to talk to me. I see a lot of guys like this when sex is talked about in church. Most of them have

---

2. I made that up. She didn't say that, but that's what I pretended to hear.

grown up in the church. Either they struggle with porn, or they're having a hard time abstaining from sex with their girlfriend. (See, you're not alone.)

So this guy walked up and said, "Here is my challenge. I've been dating this girl for four years. We love each other, and we're going to get married. We've been struggling to remain pure, and we've even talked about getting married—but my parents would flip out if we did that before finishing grad school. We've made a commitment to start obeying God in this area of our lives. But I just ... I don't know how we're going to do this. I don't know what we're going to do."

I told him, "Well, I'll tell you your options here. You're not going to like either one. Option one, you can say that for the next two or three years you're just going to be patient and pure and committed to doing things God's way. But you're going to have a really hard time with that. It's going to add a ton of pressure to your relationship. It's going to be difficult. There's probably going to be a lot of guilt and blame, and it's going to be tough on your relationship."

I said, "Your other option is that you decide you're getting married and you set a date for the summer, eight months from now. You know you want to get married. And yeah, Mom and Dad may not love that, but they'll be okay. You may be poor at first, right? It's fun to be young and married and poor. That's what ramen noodles are for. And it'll be okay."

As we were talking, I tried to imagine the rest of this kid's scenario. His parents were probably lifelong Christians. He'd probably grown up going to every church function and worship service. He'd probably known all along what the Bible says about sexual intimacy, yet for the last four years he'd been in an intimate relationship. But still, he and his girlfriend really want to start new. They want to make a commitment together. I just assumed all this right off the bat, so I didn't mince words. I know what it's like to be in a dating relationship at that age, and guys like that need to hear it straightforward.

But then he said, "Well, I just became a Christian a couple of weeks ago, so all this is new to me."

I tried not to let my eyes go wide, but I was floored. This guy was a newborn Christian. He was experiencing AHA in this area of his life for the first time ever—and he was already jumping into action! As we talked some more, he clearly recognized that it wasn't going to be easy. But here's what he said: "I know I want to do what God wants me to do, no matter what that is."

He knew there was no way to perfect the plan. He knew his parents wouldn't necessarily agree with his decision. He knew there wasn't a way to tie a bow around his scenario. But he also knew what God wanted him to do. Even though the situation was complicated, the game plan was simple.

I'm not saying you should necessarily get married right away. But what action do you need to take? You may be surprised how something as simple as making a phone call, scheduling an appointment, installing a filter, cutting up a credit card, or unfriending a Facebook friend can be a step toward your journey home.

Little Guy, Big Change

One of my favorite AHA stories in the Bible is about Zacchaeus. You can find it in Luke 19. You remember: "Zacchaeus was a wee little man, and a wee little man was he." Yeah, that guy. Jesus was passing through Jericho, where Zacchaeus lived and worked as the chief tax collector. He was superrich—like the richest guy in town. We're talking vacation homes and a fleet of Italian sports cars, if they had existed back then.

And we know this guy was really short. So picture Zacchaeus in this big crowd with elbows flying around his face as all these rubber-neckers jockeyed for a view of Jesus. Zacchaeus finally gave up trying to compete and climbed a tree. When Jesus came by, He looked up and said, "Hey, Zach, come down immediately. I must stay at your house today."

Well, the crowd started to mutter, "What! Jesus is going to be the guest of a sinner!" It wasn't because Zacchaeus had money that they called him a sinner. It was because of *how* he got his money. Remember Bernie Madoff, the Wall Street broker who ran a ginormous pyramid scheme that included a lot of rich and powerful people and millions of dollars? He's in jail now. Zacchaeus was kind of the Bernie Madoff of his day.

Here's how it worked: Jewish tax collectors would go out on behalf of the Roman government—the ruling enemy—and take money from the Israelites, their own people. They'd say, "Taxes this year are a hundred and fifty bucks." And they'd give a hundred bucks to the Romans and pocket fifty for themselves. If you were the chief tax collector, you'd also get a percentage from all the other tax collectors. So Zacchaeus got rich stealing from his own people. Not a way to get popular. He wasn't just a sinner; he sinned for a living.

Just to clarify, the Bible makes it clear that cheating and stealing don't go over well with God. With Him, morality is more important than prosperity. In other words, God cares less about how much you've got and more about how you got it and what you do with it. And everybody knew this. The people knew this. Zacchaeus knew this. Jesus knew this.

But Jesus came along and said, "Zacchaeus, let's go eat at your house." Zacchaeus was thrilled. It was an honor to host this visiting rabbi. And my guess is that Zacchaeus wasn't used to having company over for dinner. He was used to eating really well but eating alone. Nobody showed up to make small talk over a meal at Zacchaeus's house.

But something happened during this meal that changed Zacchaeus's heart. Here was someone who had accumulated tons of money and tried to find some kind of satisfaction. But happiness was always a moving target. He would get to a certain level and think, *Well, it's not here yet—maybe when I get to the next level.* Nothing worked, but he kept chasing happiness by chasing more money and possessions. Then he met Jesus and said, "This is it! This is what I have been looking for." He had this sudden awakening because of his encounter with Jesus. He realized that what he was looking for wasn't something he could order off the Internet or add to his bank account. Zacchaeus met Jesus and realized He was where true riches were found.

But there was some brutal honesty that Zacchaeus had to face. The reality was that he'd turned his back on his own people. Poor people had become poorer because of his actions. Peasants had skipped meals because of Zacchaeus. Cheaters had cheated people more because of him. He had stolen, and his fellow Israelites had suffered because of it. Zacchaeus couldn't blame anyone else. He had to look at his life with honesty, and he had to take responsibility for it.

And he did. In the face of the honest truth, he told Jesus, "I'll give half of my possessions to the poor, and I'll pay back anyone I've cheated four times that amount."

Wow, can you imagine what kind of statement that made to the people in the community?

Imagine it this way. Imagine you own a Toyota Corolla, and it's missing from your driveway one day. Someone has stolen it. But then three or four years later, you walk out and there's a Mercedes-Benz in your driveway—with this note: "Look, three or four years ago I stole your Toyota Corolla. Since then I've become a Christian. Jesus has changed my life. I'm trying to make things right. This was my Mercedes; now it's yours." What would you say? You'd go in the house and say, "Mom and Dad, we're going to church this weekend. I'm driving."

I'm guessing the people who were so upset about Jesus going to eat with the chief sinner felt a little differently now. They would have been amazed!

When our AHA experience finds its fulfillment in immediate action, Jesus is ultimately glorified. Most of the non-Christians you know are probably aware of what you say and believe. And I bet they would say that most Christians don't experience AHA; they just experience AH. But if Jesus is really in our lives and His Spirit is truly inside us, that should make the difference between AH and AHA.

When the people in Jericho saw Zacchaeus transformed, they knew it could only be because of Jesus. The same is true in our lives. Our friends have probably seen us struggle with making wise choices in different areas. But when AHA results in immediate action, they recognize something happening. They see that it wasn't by our power or determination. It was because of Jesus.

Here's the phrase I want you to pay attention to in Zacchaeus's story. In Luke 19:8, just before Zacchaeus announced his plan, he said, "Here and now I give ..."

Here and now.

I'm not gonna wait till later. I'm not gonna put it off. *Here and now* I'm gonna be generous.

That's your challenge—to take immediate action. To start *here and now*.

[CONCLUSION NEEDED HERE]

Yep, this note is supposed to be here too. It's only you who can finish this chapter. Only you can take the action you need to.

At the end of Zacchaeus's story, Jesus told him, "Today salvation has come to this house, because this man, too, is a son of Abraham. For the Son of Man came to seek and to save the lost" (Luke 19:9–10).

I've been blessed to hear and read hundreds of AHA stories over the years. And I've noticed that while they may differ in many ways, people tell them in a similar way. Most all of them include a certain time and a certain place.

I was in my living room that afternoon ...

We were at church later that weekend ...

I sat in my car early that morning ...

Most of us remember the time and place, because in that moment, we stopped putting off the change and allowed Jesus to change us in the here and now. It's what Jesus does. He changed the heart of Zacchaeus, and He can change our hearts as well. But it needs to start *here* and *now*.

Shakespeare wrote, "Tomorrow, and tomorrow, and tomorrow ... have lighted fools / The way to dusty death."[3] If there's an awakening and you come to your senses and you know something needs to be done and you think to yourself, *Tomorrow I will ...* or *next week I'm going to ...*, that's not the Holy Spirit. This was actually an awakening for me a few years ago, an AHA moment that came as I studied the Bible. I came to the startling realization that the Holy Spirit always says *today*. He never says *tomorrow*.

So how will you finish this chapter? What will be your story of taking action?

I'll get you started:

Here and now I ...

---

3. William Shakespeare, *Macbeth* (New York: New American Library, 1998), 90.

Chapter 12

DEFEATISM—IT'S TOO LATE NOW

I got a call from a lady in our church whose elderly mother was dying of pancreatic cancer. Her mother, Paulette, didn't have much time left, days at most. The daughter told me Paulette hadn't been to church since she was a young girl. It had probably been around sixty years since she had spoken to a pastor. But Paulette wanted someone to talk to her about Jesus. I said I'd be honored.

When I walked in, it was clear that Paulette's disease had taken a terrible toll. She was too frail and weak to walk; she slouched forward in her wheelchair.

Her husband was there and in good health. He immediately made it clear that he was not a Christian, and he had no intention of becoming one. He belonged to a different kind of faith. "Give me thirty days, and I'll convert you," he said and smiled. I liked him right away.

He left Paulette and me alone, and I began to explain, "The Bible says we've all sinned, Paulette." That's hard to say to an elderly

woman who is dying, but I knew she already knew this. When someone wants to talk to a pastor days before her death, there are some
things that need to be made right.

So I said, "I've sinned; you've sinned. The Bible says that the cost
of our sin is death. That's the punishment we deserve. But there's
great news. The Bible teaches that God loved the world so much that
He sent His only Son to pay that price. If we put our trust in Him,
we'll have eternal life. Jesus came to this earth and died on a cross
to forgive us. He took our punishment for us. So when you trust in
Jesus as Lord and Savior, you are forgiven. You can't save yourself, no
matter how much good you do in this life. It's a free gift that comes
from God through Jesus. In Him there's a fresh start, a new beginning, the promise of eternal life."

Paulette began to cry, but not the emotional tears of someone
who has finally come home from the Distant Country. Paulette was
disturbed by something. Her head was bowed and her gaze was low.
"I just wish it wasn't too late for me," she said. "I've had my chances,
but what can I do now? It's too late."

Too ...

Many of us hear the gospel the way Paulette heard it that day. We
hear that God sent Jesus to die for us and to offer us new life, but
we add the condition that we must accept this gift within a certain
time frame. We think the offer will expire if our sin count exceeds a
certain number or if our bill in the Distant Country gets too high.
We see the mess we're in, but we let defeatism overwhelm us. We tell
ourselves, "It's too late now."

My friend is too angry.

My parents' trust is too far gone.

My reputation is too destroyed.

My addiction is too powerful.

My life is too messed up.

Life can reach a point where it feels like things have gone too far. There are too many broken pieces to put back together. The Prodigal Son must have felt that way. Things were way past fixing. But eventually he must have decided that he didn't have anything to lose. He had no money left. He had no friends left. He had no physical strength left. He had no options left. Sometimes that's the best place to be. Sometimes that's what it takes to experience AHA—though it doesn't have to be.

If there was ever a man who must have thought it was too late, it's the man crucified next to Jesus. The Bible tells us there were two criminals hanging on crosses on either side of Jesus. They both mocked him, but something happened to one of the two criminals. He experienced AHA as he was dying next to Jesus. Here's how the Bible describes it:

> One of the criminals who hung there hurled insults at him: "Aren't you the Messiah? Save yourself and us!"
>
> But the other criminal rebuked him. "Don't you fear God," he said, "since you are under the same sentence? We are punished justly, for we are getting what our deeds deserve. But this man has done nothing wrong."

Then he said, "Jesus, remember me when you come into your kingdom."

Jesus answered him, "Truly I tell you, today you will be with me in paradise." (Luke 23:39–43)

Do you see it? There was a sudden awakening. The one guy really saw who Jesus was. There was brutal honesty as he admitted that he was getting what he deserved. And then he took action. He defended Jesus and cried out to Him for help. With his dying breath, he asked God to save him.

What made him think it wasn't too late? He was a convicted criminal dying for his crimes. He had no time left to make things right. He couldn't pay back anything to his victims.

What had this criminal witnessed that made the difference? He heard Jesus cry, "My God, my God, why have You forsaken me?" (Matt. 27:46). Was that what changed him? For the first time in infinity, Jesus didn't share perfect fellowship with His Father. The apostle Paul wrote, "God made him who had no sin to be sin for us, so that in him we might become the righteousness of God" (2 Cor. 5:21). That means all the sins of the world that were heaped on Jesus separated Him from His Father. He was separated so we could be united. But was this what transformed the thief that day? I doubt it.

The criminal also heard Jesus speak to His mother. She was watching from not far away with John the disciple. Jesus was enduring the most excruciating pain imaginable, and He asked John to take care of His mother. That was selfless love, but I don't think it changed the criminal's heart.

I think it was the prayer Jesus prayed for the soldiers who crucified Him. He hung on the cross because soldiers abused Him and nailed Him up there. But He didn't pray for their destruction or punishment. He asked God to forgive them.

This thief had suffered the same abuse from the same soldiers. He must have hated them. But what do you do with grace that says, "Father, forgive them"? I think it destroyed this thief. His heart melted in that moment. *Who is this guy who speaks forgiveness to His own executioners? Maybe it's not too late for me after all.*

Just the Right Time

I reached over and grabbed Paulette's hand. At that point she wasn't the only one crying. "Oh no, no," I said. "It's just the right time. It is never too late with Jesus." And in her living room we prayed. She repented and confessed and gave her life to Jesus. It was a beautiful moment as she was baptized with her daughter and granddaughter watching. She was determined to be baptized to express her new faith even though she was very weak physically. Paulette inspired me. It takes a lot of courage to get to the end of the road, realize it's a dead end, and still be willing to turn around.

The Prodigal Son reached his own dead end, and he took action. He got up. But on his journey home, he must have played the scene over and over in his mind: What would he say? What would his father do? How bad would his punishment be?

The son didn't expect much. He had been humbled and was ready to own up to his mistakes. But he was hoping that at the very best, his dad would let him become a servant. He knew he had disowned his family. He had taken the money and run and basically said, "You're dead to me." He expected his father to say the same to him.

Many of us assume our relationship with God is measured in a kind of quantitative calculation. And so the word *enough* can haunt many Christians. At some point, things feel too far gone, and we know we can't do enough to even out the scales. We look at our lives, tally up our rights and our wrongs, and face the defeating truth: we can never do enough. We can't out-right our wrongs. There isn't enough time or ability to make things right, so we end up doing nothing. The time for action comes and goes. So with our heads bowed and eyes low, we say, "It's too late now." We are defeated.

Trying Only Makes It Worse

Last summer my family had the opportunity to house-sit for some friends who owned an aboveground pool. In the heat of summer, we were ready to veg out and cool off in the water.

But the first morning, my wife said, "I think there may be a leak in the pool. I'm pretty sure the water level dropped during the night." I went to investigate, and sure enough, the water level was six or eight inches lower. I examined the outside of the pool, but I couldn't find a leak. I was going to have to get in the pool to find the leak. This meant I needed some goggles, but all I could find were my son's green goggles. They suctioned onto my face like two sea urchins and cut off the circulation to my head. Still I dove in and started looking for the leak. Sure enough, there was a hole near the bottom of the pool about the size of a pencil eraser. Water was steadily leaking out, but it wasn't too bad, so I didn't feel a sense of urgency.

I climbed out and plopped onto a lawn chair. *Maybe we can wait till our friends get back and they can handle it,* I thought. But the more I thought about it, the more it bugged me. So I headed to the pool store and explained the situation. They sold me a round patch and an adhesive. "You smear this glue on the patch, swim down to the spot, and press it gently against the edges of the hole," the pool guy said. "Not a big deal."

So I went home, strapped on the green goggles, smeared the glue on the patch, swam down to the leak, and started pressing gently against the hole. Not a big deal.

But one second I was pressing gently to plug a leak the size of an eraser, and the next second my hand was being sucked through a vortex the size of a basketball. And not just my hand, but eighteen thousand gallons of water. My brain told my arm to yank back, but there was too much water pushing down on me. Terrifyingly, I couldn't pull out. A thought struck: *I'm gonna drown in my buddy's aboveground pool.* Desperate not to become someone else's sermon illustration, I pushed off the bottom and managed to climb out. Panicked and overdosed on adrenaline, I ran and grabbed towels and pathetically attempted to stuff them in the hole. Bulging with towels and under pressure from running water, the hole ripped wider. Finally I just stood there with the punishing realization that there was nothing I could do. I watched eighteen thousand gallons of water empty into my buddy's backyard.

The goggles were halfway down my face. My mouth was open. My eyes were wide. My kids came out and were shocked. My son had tears in his eyes. My teenage daughter said what all of us were thinking: "Did that really just happen?"

I wish this story had some kind of happy ending, but it doesn't. I didn't even get a refund on the patch. My attempt was a complete failure. I single-handedly turned a small leak into a full-blown disaster.

I think it's worth acknowledging that some of us have tried to patch things up before, and it hasn't ended well. We've acted with good intentions, but our attempts to fix our problems have only made them worse. We've tried to reconcile a relationship, but it has ended in hurtful words that we regret. We've set boundaries and distanced ourselves from temptation, but the relapse seems unavoidable. We get back up, determined to do better, but only fall harder. Eventually we reach the point where we say to ourselves, "It's too late now." After trying everything we can to patch the hole, we finally give up and watch helplessly.

You may be reading and thinking, *I've tried to change, and it's never worked. It's too late.* But let me ask you a few questions:

- When you tried to patch things up, did you try it your way or God's way?
- When you made an attempt to start over, was it on your terms or God's?
- When you last tried to act, did you take the time to be brutally honest with yourself and with God, or did you try to skip straight to action?
- When you tried to stick with it, was it with your own power or with the power of the Holy Spirit?

• When you acted, was it motivated by guilt and
shame or by the love and grace of Jesus?

A Lot to Atone For

You probably remember hearing Tiger Woods's apology a few years
ago. He had his awakening—a 9 iron to the head usually does the
job. He had his honesty—every magazine cover on the rack told
the brutal truth. And for fifteen minutes he laid out his plan of
action, telling the world what he was going to do. In his interview
Tiger mentioned his Buddhist faith. Buddhists have an eightfold
path, a religious walk based solely on an individual's performance.
If you can live a good enough life, you can rack up enough points
to reach enlightenment and a heavenly bliss called Nirvana. And
because it's all about being good enough, there's always a lot to
do. You could hear that in Tiger's speech. He talked a lot about
the action he would need to take. Here are some of the phrases he
used:

> *I have a lot to atone for …*
> *It's now up to me …*
> *I have a long way to go …*
> *I am the one who needs to change …*
> *I have a lot of work to do …*

As I listened to Tiger, I thought a lot about the parable of the
prodigal son. What's interesting is that there's a similar story told in
Buddhist literature. At least the two stories start out similarly.

In both stories, a young man rebels against his father, goes off to a distant land, and has everything fall apart. They experience pretty severe consequences for their decisions.

In both stories, the guy decides he wants to come home and be reconciled with his father. They both make the journey home to own up for their mistakes.

From there the two stories go in different directions.

In the Buddhist story the father forces the son to pay the penalty for his misdeeds by spending years as a servant shoveling excrement—that's a fancy word for poop.

In Jesus's story everything depends on the father's response. And everyone in His first-century audience thought the father was going to let his son have it. At the very least, that boy was going to be shoveling poop until he'd paid back his father—with interest.

We read the son's action: "So he got up and went to his father" (Luke 15:20).

But what will the father's action be?

Defeating Defeatism

A spirit of defeatism can be expected if everything depends on us. If it's up to our actions to save ourselves, then, yeah, it's too late—way too late. A spirit of defeatism comes because we don't accurately take into account how the Father will respond when we come home.

Here's how Jesus told it:

> But while he was still a long way off, his father saw
> him and was filled with compassion for him; he ran

to his son, threw his arms around him and kissed him.

The son said to him, "Father, I have sinned against heaven and against you. I am no longer worthy to be called your son."

But the father said to his servants, "Quick! Bring the best robe and put it on him. Put a ring on his finger and sandals on his feet. Bring the fattened calf and kill it. Let's have a feast and celebrate. For this son of mine was dead and is alive again; he was lost and is found." So they began to celebrate. (Luke 15:20–24)

Two parts of this story would have been especially shocking to Jesus's audience.

1. The son's request for his inheritance while the father was still living. His action said, "I wish you were dead. I don't want you; I want your money."
2. The father's response. Even more shocking than the son's blatant disrespect and coldhearted selfishness were the undeserved grace and extravagant love of his father when the son returned. The way Jesus described it was scandalous.

I love the phrase *while he was still a long way off.* The son still had a long way to go before he made it home. But his father didn't wait.

God doesn't wait for you to make it home on your own either. In fact, before you even thought about taking action, God had already acted. The Bible says, "While we were still sinners, Christ died for us" (Rom. 5:8). While we were still living it up in the Distant Country, God acted.

It was also shocking that the father ran to his son. Back in that day, Jewish patriarchs didn't run. A patriarch would never hike up his robe and take off running. It wasn't sophisticated. It wasn't refined.

But this father made up lost ground. And when he reached his son, he threw his arms around him and kissed him. He didn't wait for his son to get cleaned up. He gave his sweaty, stinking, pig-sitting son a big bear hug and kisses. The father loved his son just as he was.

We think, *It's too late now. I don't have time to get cleaned up. I don't have time to get my life together.* But it's not too late—the Father wants you just the way you are. When you finally act, your heavenly Father comes running with arms wide open. He loves you just as you are, but He doesn't leave you that way. He puts His best robe on your dirty body. He puts the family ring on your hand. He kills the fattened calf.

Meat was a rare delicacy during Jesus's time. It might get served at a party, but nothing was more extravagant than killing a fat calf.

Do you see how quickly the focus of the story shifts from the action of the son to the action of the father? We make the story all about us, and it feels too late. But the story is really about the Father. And it's never too late.

AHA.

Celebrate

My friend agreed to share his AHA story:

Eight years ago I left home and went away to Colorado State University. I joined a fraternity and majored in partying. For the first three semesters, I never stopped to think about what I was doing. I never prayed. But then reality came crashing down on me; I could no longer deny what was happening. I flunked four of my five classes. It was a wake-up call. I knew I needed to make some changes. I needed to get out of the fraternity and lose some of my friends. But what I really needed was to change my relationship with God, if He would still have me.

There was no place for privacy in the frat house, so I took a phone into a bathroom to call my parents and explain that I had failed. There was a stack of pornography, and I didn't want to look in that direction, so I sat on top of it. I explained to my parents that I had blown it in a lot of areas of my life, not just my grades, but also in my walk with Christ. I had strayed away from Him. My parents listened, and then they said three words to me.

They didn't say, "Turn things around."

They didn't say, "Make things right."

They didn't say, "Get some help."

They didn't say, "Figure it out."
They didn't say, "We love you."
They didn't say, "We forgive you."
It was better than that. They said:
"Just come home."

The story of the Prodigal Son who came to his senses, told himself the hard truth, got up, and went home to his father's open arms ends with this beautiful conclusion:

"So they began to celebrate."

Chapter 13

LOST IN THE FATHER'S HOUSE—THE FINAL AHA

The camera pans across a long road, where a young man walks. Zooming in, we can see that this guy is wearing torn clothing. He's caked with mud.

Cut to a wide shot of a hazy horizon. We see the man crest the horizon. But suddenly the weary figure is blocked from view—another figure has run into the frame. There's nothing but sandals and a flowing robe on the screen.

Cut to a new view of the road as this new figure, clearly an older man, runs full speed toward the young guy.

Cut to a close-up as the two embrace. The younger man, solemn faced and holding back tears, tries to communicate a grave message to the older man. But the older man doesn't seem to hear him. He kisses the young man, and tears of joy stream down his face. He looks back and calls to someone offscreen.

Cut to a courtyard filled with people. Tables are spread full of food. But every eye is on a large table in the corner. The camera zooms in on the young man, now wearing a fancy robe. He's smiling and watching as the older man stands at the head of this table and addresses the crowd. He raises his glass.

Cut to a shot over the man's shoulder as all the guests are raising their glasses, toasting along with him, and applauding.

Cut to a slow pull from the party. The camera dollies out of the courtyard, and the light from the party grows smaller. The revelers grow more distant, though no less enthusiastic. The camera slowly fades to black.

Roll credits.

After the Credits Roll

Do you sit and watch the credits roll at the end of a movie? Do you read as the producer, director, assistant director, actors, and a host of others who contributed to the film are listed—everyone from the makeup artist to the catering company? Probably not. I mean, I respect film professionals, and I know it takes a huge team to pull off any major production, but that doesn't mean I sit in a dark theater waiting to see who was the key grip while everyone else has to squeeze past to exit the aisle.

The only time I sit through the credits is when there's a post-cedits scene. You think the movie is over, but it isn't. If you're a fan of superhero movies, you know what I mean. Sometimes these scenes are really teasers of the next movie in the series. Other times they're just for fun, like when the Avengers eat shawarma together.

But in Jesus's day, movies hadn't been invented. The listeners heard Jesus tell of the celebration at the son's return, and they probably thought, *The End*. I imagine Jesus finished His sentence about the celebration, and then kind of paused. The listeners would have nodded their heads, showing they were intrigued by this interesting story. Everyone likes a happy ending, right? "So they began to celebrate" even sounds an awful lot like "and they lived happily ever after."

But then Jesus cleared His throat and used a classic transitional word in storytelling. It's a word that lets listeners know the story is not over. It's the kind of word that reminds us, in a novel, that there is a parallel plot unfolding. Storytellers love this word, and Jesus put it to excellent use. Everyone thought the story was over; then Jesus cleared His throat and said, "Meanwhile ..."

Attentive listeners might remember that Jesus began the story with a brief but important detail: "There was a man who had two sons." After that, the focus was all on the younger son and his father. But when we come to the celebration scene, there was no older brother to be found.

Cut to a flashback of earlier that day. The camera rolls across a nearby field, where a man works the ground tirelessly. A close-up reveals a family resemblance between him and the younger son and the father. He is the older brother, faithfully tending his father's lands. As the sun sets beyond the field, the older brother hears a commotion at the family compound. He calls to someone offscreen, and a young servant walks into the frame. The servant excitedly explains the return of the younger son and the father's celebration. Then the older brother loses it. The camera pulls in on his face. His eyes are a tempest of emotions. Confusion, hurt, and anger swirl into defiant rage. The brother turns back to the field, coldly refusing to go to the celebration with the servant.

Cut to the party. The camera pulls away from the festivities and pans across the moonlit field. The moving frame reveals a silhouetted figure, standing alone. Cut to a close-up of the older brother. His face forms a confused grimace; his arms are folded in frustration.

Cut to a wide shot of the field. Another figure comes into view, walking slowly toward the older brother. The father has come to plead with the older brother to come celebrate his brother's homecoming.

But the older brother says, "Look! All these years I've been slaving for you and never disobeyed your orders. Yet you never gave me even a young goat so I could celebrate with my friends. But when this son of yours who has squandered your property with prostitutes comes home, you kill the fattened calf for him!" (Luke 15:29–30).

Older Bros

Don't miss this: The older brother never left his father. He never broke the rules. He never went to a distant country. But he never experienced AHA.

Which story is more tragic—the younger son who lost everything and ended up in a pigpen but experienced AHA? Or the older son who responsibly lived at home with his father, followed all the rules, but never experienced AHA?

The older brother didn't get it, and he was disappointed in his father. He was disgusted by the extravagant grace shown to his brother. He felt like the situation demanded an explanation. It seems the older brother was expecting what some of Jesus's listeners were expecting: justice for the sinner.

To really understand the point of this parable, you have to look back at the beginning of Luke 15 to see who was listening when Jesus told it. Half of the audience was tax collectors and sinners. And spiritually speaking, they are the younger brother. They are far from the Father, living in the Distant Country.

But the other half of Jesus's crowd was Pharisees and teachers of the law. These are the older brother. They spent their days studying the Scriptures and explaining what they meant—important stuff. And they looked down on Jesus for spending time with the dirty younger brother.

So Jesus used this older brother to speak to them. He knew the challenge of being an older brother is that you almost never see yourself as the older brother. He created a character who had done everything right, a son who had been faithful and worked hard for his father's benefit. That's how many of the Pharisees would have seen themselves. These men literally worked in the Father's house—at the temple—but their hearts were far from Him.

What was their problem? Their understanding of God was fundamentally flawed. They saw Him as harsh and unforgiving. They viewed God as a cosmic cop, patrolling the universe and waiting for people to mess up so He could bust them and hand out an eternal verdict.

My brother-in-law is a police officer. Anyone related to a policeman knows that his stories trump everybody else's. My story about discovering the original Greek word for *poop*[1] is never going to beat

---

1. The word is *skubala*, by the way, and is used in Philippians 3:8.

his story about rappelling down from a helicopter to torch illegal fields of marijuana.

One time he was telling me about some serious accident scenes he had come upon.

"They must be relieved when you show up on the scene," I said. "People must feel a lot better when they see you pull up."

"Not really," he said. "A lot of times they're pretty nervous, because when I come on the scene, I'm there to investigate. I'm there to assign blame. I'm there to hand out punishments and discipline. They get a little nervous when I come around." He paused for a minute, then added, "But they're always glad to see the paramedics. See, the paramedics come in, and their job is to free those who are trapped, bandage those who have been wounded, and help those who are hurting."

The Pharisees listening to Jesus were about to learn what they had forgotten—and what we often forget: the followers of Jesus aren't on earth to assign blame; we're here to free the trapped, bandage the wounded, help the hurting, and celebrate homecomings.

AHA.

But the older son didn't get it. He stayed angry and offended, despite his father's pleas. This older bro may have worked hard and faithfully tended the fields, but he was lost in his father's house.

There was no awakening.

There was no honesty.

There was no action.

The truth is, he, too, was a prodigal son. He, too, had a heart that was far from his father. He, too, was lost—but he didn't see it.

Pastor Tim Keller puts it this way: "The bad son was lost in his badness, but the good son was lost in his goodness."[2]

You may never have been to a Distant Country. You may have an impressive religious résumé. You may have followed all the rules. You may have read this entire book thinking of all the people you know in the Distant Country who really need to hear it. But are you the one Jesus has been talking to all along?

Since older brothers have a hard time seeing themselves as someone in need of of AHA—I know because I've been there—I want to give you a few descriptions of what an older brother is like:

Critical of Others' Badness

Older brothers are good at focusing on other people's flaws. They don't want to recognize any changes in prodigals because they can't see past the mistakes. Instead of encouraging and supporting people who try to make a truthful turnaround, an older brother keeps bringing up their past lies. Older bros often have a hard time celebrating when AHA happens because they're busy criticizing other people's badness.

When others come home from the Distant Country, broken and wanting to do things differently, do you cross your arms instead of opening them? Do you say things like, "Let's give it some time," or "Well, you need to make some things right," or "They need to get their act together." If you refuse to celebrate when your brothers and sisters come home from the Distant Country, it's a good sign that you're missing AHA in your own life—and that you're more lost than they are because you're lost at home.

---

2. Timothy Keller, *The Prodigal God* (New York: Penguin, 2008).

See, nobody asked you. This isn't your house. It's the *Father's* house. You don't get to decide who is allowed to come home and be called sons and daughters. When we refuse to celebrate, it shows that we've missed it. We've missed God's grace in our own lives. We've overlooked or forgotten what we've been saved from. If we could clearly see our own sin, we would be the first ones to celebrate. We would grab the Father's robe and run right behind Him, because we know what He's done for us. And when we live with an awareness of what God has done for us—oh, man—our arms are wide open.

Confident in One's Own Goodness

A second sign of older-brother syndrome is confidence in your own goodness instead of the Father's grace. The older brother was quick to point out to the father, "All these years I've been slaving for you and have never disobeyed your orders." He was really saying, "Look what I deserve. I've been good. I've followed the rules. I've done what I'm supposed to. I deserve your blessing. I've earned it."

This kind of claim is all about him, not about his father's care and provision in his life. See, the older brother lived a life fully dependent on his father. But he didn't even acknowledge the father's generosity. Instead, he threw a spoiled fit. "It's not fair!" he complained. "I've never even received a small goat to party with my friends."

I don't think these were brand-new feelings for the older bro. After years of working hard for his father, he felt proud of his work ethic and discipline. His resentment probably started when his father gave the younger son half the inheritance, and since then, he'd been keeping score. And now this? A party for the stupid rebel?

The problem with pride about our own goodness is that it feeds the attitude that we deserve something from the Father, that we're earning something. But God's house is not a house of merit; it's a house of mercy.

The older brother claims, "I've never disobeyed." The younger brother says, "I'm not worthy." One brother demands what he deserves. The other begs for mercy. One brother sulks in frustration; the other celebrates in joy. Focusing on our own spiritual résumés divides our spiritual family. The father and Prodigal Son celebrated while the older brother stayed alone in the field. But God doesn't withhold mercy or stop the party just because one of His children disagrees. So until you go from "I've never disobeyed" to "I'm not worthy," you will not have AHA.

Too Tough?

I know this sounds harsh toward the older brother. You may be thinking, *If Jesus is so merciful, why is He so tough on the Pharisees?* That's a fair question.

Here's what I think: Jesus knows that most people base what they think about God on His representatives. In that day, people viewed God based on how the Pharisees and teachers lived and behaved. Think about it: Our interactions with employees shape our view of a company. I mean, if you walk into Target and a sales representative is rude and cusses at you, you're not going to be happy. You might complain to him personally, but more likely, you or your parents are going to say, "I'd like to speak to the manager, please."

That's what's behind Jesus's challenge to these Pharisees. These older brothers lived and worked in the Father's house. They told the people how to follow the Father. Jesus knew the people were looking to them as a reference point of what the Father is like. And He knew there were a lot of older brothers totally misrepresenting the heart of God. (There still are.) These older bros were portraying God as a Father who is unreasonable, unpleasable, uncaring, and unmerciful. And it's often the older brothers' portrayal of God that sends prodigals to the Distant Country in the first place.

But that's not the kind of Father Jesus described.

The Final AHA

After the older brother went off, his father responded—not with anger but with gentleness.

> "My son," the father said, "you are always with me, and everything I have is yours. But we had to celebrate and be glad, because this brother of yours was dead and is alive again; he was lost and is found." (Luke 15:31–32)

Jesus revealed the heart of the father and our heavenly Father. He wants us. He wants relationship with the younger and older sons, with you and with me. And the Father knows exactly what each of His children needs. He knows what the prodigal needs. He knows what the older brother needs. He knows what I need. He knows what you need. And He knows just how to reach us if we'll let Him.

As Jesus ends His powerful story, He revealed two important truths about the Father:

The Father Seeks Out Both Sons

Both sons were in the wrong, and it was really their responsibility to seek out the father. The younger son did, and the father was waiting. As soon as he could see his son on the horizon, he ran to him. He didn't sit back and wait. He didn't make his son sweat out each last step. He didn't posture himself as most patriarchs would have back then, full of pride and indignant about any disrespect. No, he ran to his son.

And when the older brother was in the field, the father left the celebration to find him. He engaged his son even when he didn't have to.

What do both of these interactions tell us about God?

He longs for a relationship with His children.

A friend of mine told me about an elderly man he knew who could no longer take care of himself. His family made the difficult decision to put him in a nursing home. But every Sunday afternoon, the man's daughter and her husband and their children would go see him. So every Sunday this elderly man would wait for his daughter and her family to visit. He looked forward to it all week and was always out waiting for them. But as the years passed, his mind grew more feeble and weak. He had a hard time remembering the children's names. He sometimes had trouble getting back to his room. But no matter what, he was always there waiting on Sunday afternoons.

One day the daughter asked, "Daddy, do you know what day of the week it is?" Her father couldn't tell her. So the daughter asked, "Well, Daddy, how did you know to wait for us today?"

He answered, "Oh, honey, I wait for you every day."

God is a loving Father who longs for His children to come home. On the day you finally come home, you'll find Him waiting for you. You might wonder, *How did He know I was coming today?* He has been waiting for you every day.

The Father Is Loving and Gracious with Both Sons

The father had every right to come down hard on each of his sons. They deserved it. The people listening to this parable would have agreed that the father was well within his rights to deal out justice and punishment to both sons.

But after the younger son's insulting choices and reckless living, the father embraced him with kisses and hugs.

And after the older brother's harsh words and disrespect, the father lovingly explained himself. An Israelite patriarch would never have had to explain himself. Households then were not democracies; they were dictatorships. Yet this father answered his older son's anger with patience and grace.

A pastor friend of mine told me about a sixteen-year-old girl in his church who became pregnant. She was the daughter of a local businessman and church leader. She and her boyfriend came to the pastor, scared and not knowing what to do.

"Have you told your father?" my friend asked.

She shook her head no. She was afraid of what her father would do.

The couple kept meeting with the pastor, but she refused to tell her father. She knew she was beginning to show, and she couldn't keep it a secret much longer. She went to see the pastor one last time and told him her plan. She and her boyfriend were running away together. After they were far enough away, she wanted the pastor to tell her father the story.

My friend pleaded with her to tell her dad, but she was too scared. My friend insisted, "Let's go together right now and tell him. I'll be by your side." Before she could disagree, the pastor ushered her out the door and straight to her dad's office. The secretary said he was on the phone, but my friend said, "I'm sorry, but this can't wait." They walked right in and sat down at the father's desk.

The father saw his pastor, his daughter, and the tears. "I'll call you back," he said immediately. As soon as he hung up the phone, the girl started sobbing. She tried to speak, but words wouldn't come out.

Finally the pastor said, "Your daughter has something she'd like to tell you."

The father turned his gaze to his daughter, who wouldn't look at him. He exhaled with emotion and said, "I hope you're not here to tell me you're pregnant."

The girl started sobbing even harder and choked out, "Daddy, I didn't mean to."

My friend was startled when the father suddenly sprang from his desk, came around, and stood in front of the girl. His voice caught as he said, "You stand up! You stand up here and look me in the eye!"

She didn't move.

"I said stand up!"

My friend was already on his feet, unsure what would happen next. The girl slowly stood and, with tears streaming down her cheeks, looked at her father. He placed his hands on her shoulder and looked her square in the eyes. Then he spread out his arms and embraced his baby girl.

My friend was standing close enough that he could hear the father whisper into her ear, "It will be okay now, honey. I love you no matter what. We'll get through this together."

The Letter

We expect God to be an angry Father who demands justice. But through Jesus, God gives us love and grace when we don't deserve it. Ultimately, the story Jesus told in Luke 15 isn't about two sons who disobeyed. It's about a father who loved his children unconditionally. AHA.

I want to close this book with a letter from a mom to her prodigal son. I think it helps us understand the heart of God our Father, who waits for us, pursues us, and longs to embrace us, just the way we are.

She wrote:

I remember a boy who was so eager to call me mama and who gave spontaneous hugs and kisses. You loved to eat all of my food and made me feel like I was the best cook in the world. I remember your stubbornness and hoped you would use it to change your world. But instead it's changed you. And we miss you, the real you, the one who is strong for the weak and who makes everyone else feel safe.

I can't help but wonder if I'm somehow to blame for the change of direction you've made lately. Was I too strict? Was I not strict enough? Did I show you the love and grace that is Jesus? Was I too much of a hypocrite? I try to figure out what I would do differently if I had the chance. Would

I affirm you more and correct you less? Would I discipline you and guide you more gently?

I realize I'm trying to rewrite the past, and that can never be done, no matter how hard I try. And I remember that I should forget those things that are behind and strain toward what is ahead. But I start to worry about the now and where you are and what you're doing. And I stare at the glow of the clock in my room and wonder who you're with at 1:30 in the morning and why you're not answering your phone or texts.

But here the Comforter draws me near and whispers that I should be anxious for nothing. You see, dear heart, you don't belong to me. You never have. Your mama and your daddy gave you back to God, and I believe that He has a plan for your future and that He will finish what He started in you. And so with this letter I write to you—which you may never see—I pray that you know one thing. This one is very important. I pray that you know that my arms are wide open for your return. Any time you are ready, no matter what you've done, we'll face it together. Because God's arms are ready, too, you know? He awaits your return. He will be dancing and spinning and celebrating with the best of them. He misses you more than I do. He paid a great price to know you, and every day that you're away seems like an eternity.

So make haste, my son. We're waiting—Daddy, Jesus, and I. We are fattening the calf and preparing the party. We are standing in the yard shielding our eyes from the sun, hoping to catch a glimpse of you coming over the horizon. The day cannot come soon enough.

Arms always open,
Mama

AHA.

STUDY QUESTIONS

CHAPTER 1—THE DISTANT COUNTRY

1. Have you been to a Distant Country, or are you there now? What led you there?
2. What is your view of God? What are five to ten words you would use to describe how you honestly feel about Him?
3. When was the last time you simply said, "God, I need Your help"?

PART 1—SUDDEN AWAKENING

CHAPTER 2—COMING TO YOUR SENSES

1. Why is it so difficult for us to hear and respond to the early warning alarms God puts in our lives?
2. Can you think of a time when you ignored an alarm and faced consequences later? Looking back, what should you have done to wake up instead of pressing snooze?

3. Is there an alarm sounding in your life right now? What step(s) do you need to take to make sure you don't ignore it?

4. Pray for God to open your eyes to the ways He is trying to get your attention.

CHAPTER 3—A DESPERATE MOMENT

1. Have you ever hit rock bottom? What happened?

2. How have you responded to difficult circumstances in your life? Have they driven you *away from* God or drawn you *to* God?

3. Complete this sentence: "I stopped running from God when …"

CHAPTER 4—A STARTLING REALIZATION

1. Have you had a moment of realization when you suddenly saw what had been right in front of you for a long time?

2. How much silence and solitude do you have in your life? How can you get more of that kind of time?

3. Do you have someone in your life who has your permission to "flip the switch," to tell you that last 5 percent of truth?

PART 2—BRUTAL HONESTY

CHAPTER 5—TALKING TO YOURSELF

1. When you look into the spiritual mirror, what do you see that no one else sees? What has kept you from bringing it into the light?

2. When you think about confession, what comes to mind?

3. Do you have someone in your life who asks you the hard questions and to whom you confess sin? What would it take for you to develop that kind of relationship?

4. What would change in your life if you were willing to regularly do the hard, uncomfortable work of confession?

CHAPTER 6—DENIAL: IF I IGNORE IT, MAYBE IT WILL GO AWAY

1. What happens to us when we live in denial?

2. When we are faced with uncomfortable truth, what are the emotions we experience that lead us to denial? How can we confront them rather than giving in to them?

3. Read John 8:31–36. How does this relate to denial and confession?

CHAPTER 7—PROJECTION: IT'S NOT MY FAULT, SO IT'S NOT MY RESPONSIBILITY

1. Who or what do you tend to blame when you find yourself in "the pigpen"?

2. Why is it so difficult for us to accept fault—with no ifs, ands, or buts?

3. Are there people you need to admit fault to right now? Write out what you need to say to them, and watch for projection and subtle ways you try to excuse yourself. Then go to them and read what you've written.

CHAPTER 8—MINIMIZE: IT'S NOT THAT BIG OF A DEAL

1. Where do you see minimization in your life?

2. What is the connection between denial, projection, and minimization? Why do we so easily give in to these?

3. What can the response of the Ninevites in Jonah 3 teach us about a proper response to conviction?

4. The Prodigal Son realized that his decisions had caused significant relational damage that needed to be mended. Take a few minutes to honestly assess the relational consequences of your actions—even the actions that don't seem like that big a deal. What can you start working on to mend those relationships?

PART 3—IMMEDIATE ACTION

CHAPTER 9—TIME TO GET UP

1. What are the barriers between brutal honesty and immediate action? Why is it so difficult to pass through them?

2. Why is there often such a difference between public beliefs, private beliefs, and core beliefs? How can we begin to develop consistency?

3. As you've read through this book so far, maybe you've had a sudden awakening, and maybe you've even been brutally honest with yourself. In light of that, what action do you need to take?

4. What is standing between you and that necessary action?

CHAPTER 10—PASSIVITY: I'M SURE EVERYTHING WILL WORK ITSELF OUT

1. It seems so natural to choose the path of least resistance, but that's not what will lead us to AHA. How does the hard work of immediate action bring changes that the path of least resistance never could?

2. Passivity happens when we honor something over God. We rarely, if ever, intend for that to happen, so what leads us to honoring things like family, money, and comfort above God?

3. What's your first step? How will you act on it?

CHAPTER 11—PROCRASTINATION: I'LL GET TO IT LATER

1. What are the areas of life where you procrastinate?

2. If you look back honestly, what has procrastination cost you?

3. How do you see putting off the pain, prolonging the pleasure, and/or planning it to perfection playing a role in your procrastination?

4. Can you think back to some "here and now" moments you've experienced in the past? What led to those moments, and what changes came out of them?

CHAPTER 12—DEFEATISM: IT'S TOO LATE NOW

1. Do you feel, or have you felt, that it's too late for you? Why?

2. When has your life been like trying to plug up the hole in the bottom of a pool—the more you try to fix something, the worse it gets?

3. Have you tried to make changes before that either didn't work or didn't last long? Look back through the list of questions on 176–177. Were any of those true of you?

4. What needs to be different this time if you're truly going to experience AHA?

CHAPTER 13—LOST IN THE FATHER'S HOUSE: THE FINAL AHA

1. Do you find it easy or difficult to accept prodigals when they return home?

2. Knowing what we know about the older brother from the end of the story, can you understand his response to his brother's actions?

3. From what we've learned about AHA, what are the next steps the older brother needs to take in order to experience AHA?

4. Whether you are more of a younger brother or an older brother right now, what are your next steps toward experiencing AHA?